820.809

In the Event of Fire

(NEW WRITING SCOTLAND 27)

Edited by
Alan Bissett
and
Liz Niven

Association for Scottish Literary Studies

Association for Scottish Literary Studies
Department of Scottish Literature, 7 University Gardens
University of Glasgow, Glasgow G12 8QH
www.asls.org.uk

ASLS is a registered charity no. SC006535

First published 2009

British Library Cataloguing in Publication Data

A CIP record for this book is available
from the British Library

ISBN 978-0-948877-92-6

The Association for Scottish Literary Studies
acknowledges the support of the Scottish Arts Council
towards the publication of this book

Printed by Bell & Bain Ltd, Glasgow

CONTENTS

INTRODUCTION

This year has seen one new editor and one experienced editor share the reins of *New Writing Scotland*. Reins, it seemed sometimes, which belonged to an impatient horse. *New Writing Scotland* represents an annual jerk-forwards in the onwards motion of Scottish literature, with all its energy, raw and pulsing and unpublished. Reading through the submissions this year was a frequently exciting experience: those times, it felt good. Other times, being editor was an apologetic throwing of negativity into the world, that understanding of just how many rejections we would have to make.

Let us tell you about The Box. It sits in the corner of the room. The Box! Like a booby-trapped device in a horror movie. Will it spring open today with knives? Or flowers? Each year, *New Writing Scotland* editors report on the staggering number of entries received, but it's difficult to visualise just how huge a pile 800 of them is, just how long it takes to read. We make no grumbles: this is the editors' job and we carry it out with much determination and enthusiasm. After the reading? The monumental task of grading each anonymous submission as Yes, No or Maybe, a little intellectual beauty contest, and coming to a mutual conclusion about 800 different catwalk models, not knowing if we're giving a new writer their first taste of publication, or rejecting the work of some major literary figure.

Satisfying were those whose opening lines struck a real confident strut. Equally relished, in their own way, were the ones which could be discarded almost immediately. Most frustrating was the large body of Maybes, where talent was clear but we observed technical problems or maybe our Maybe was simply down to subjectivity. These are the manuscripts over which editors can agonise the most. Should we publish, therefore giving a writer who was close-but-not-quite-there encouragement and an audience? Or should we protect the writer from too early exposure, allowing time for further crafting? In the main, we chose the latter option, selecting those which both editors felt had achieved a certain clarity, depth or singularity of voice. These, basically, are the ones which made us most excited, made us think: yes. A double yes. Yes! This writer needs to be read.

But what of trends this year? We were surprised by the sheer volume of nature poetry submitted. Almost all of them were pretty in their own way, but had very little to *say*, as such, beyond the immediate impression of what was being looked at. It then becomes difficult to distinguish one poem from the other, without some element of surprise or subversion at work. So too for the flipside: that of urban depravation (deprivation?) stories in unconvincing dialogue. While we argue passionately for the validity of Scots writing, it has tae sound authentic. Just as happens with Standard English, when an author gets it right – syntax, phonetics, rhythm all flowing and real – an unmistakable linguistic energy is unleashed. When it goes wrong it feels like being slapped with a wet kilt.

The editors noted that very little experimental work was submitted. Perhaps this is a case of writers responding to previous content in *New Writing Scotland*, feeling that certain, safer types of aesthetic are favoured. However, writers who took risks with form or voice, even if not selected, certainly stood out from the crowd. Experimentalism wasn't *prioritised* by editors over conventional, yet more fully realised pieces, but it's refreshing when writers dare to be different.

Which leads us to our title. We like 'In the Event of Fire' for its everydayness (it's a sign which we read, perhaps literally, on a daily basis) but also for the danger implied. Notice how fire is described as *event*. Something which erupts from the ordinary. Something which we are *cautious* about. We responded to writers who abandoned caution, who let the fire become an event, who did not scream, running for the exits, but who let it burn.

Now, let it spread.

It's exit out the Fire Door for one of the current editors, her three-year editorial post being completed. It's been great reading to find out which voices will set the heather alight each year, and a weather eye will keep watching from a safe distance. Our other editor, however, very much looks forward to The Box next year sitting there in the corner of his room, ticking away with the event of fire.

Alan Bissett
Liz Niven

NEW WRITING SCOTLAND 28

The twenty-eighth volume of *New Writing Scotland* will be published in summer 2010. Submissions are invited from writers resident in Scotland or Scots by birth, upbringing or inclination. All forms of writing are welcome: autobiography and memoirs; creative responses to events and experiences; drama; graphic artwork (monochrome only); poetry; political and cultural commentary and satire; short fiction; travel writing or any other creative prose may be submitted, but not full-length plays or novels, though self-contained extracts are acceptable. The work must be neither previously published nor accepted for publication and may be in any of the languages of Scotland.

Submissions should be typed on one side of the paper only and the sheets secured at the top left corner. Prose pieces should be double-spaced and carry an approximate word-count. **You should provide a covering letter, clearly marked with your name and address. Please do not put your name or other details on the individual works.** If you would like to receive an acknowledgement of receipt of your manuscript, please enclose a stamped addressed postcard. If you would like to be informed if your submission is unsuccessful, or would like your submissions returned, you should enclose a stamped addressed envelope with sufficient postage. Submissions should be sent by **30 September 2009**, in an A4 envelope, to the address below. We are sorry but we cannot accept submissions by fax or email.

Please be aware that we have limited space in each edition, and therefore shorter pieces are more suitable – although longer items of exceptional quality may still be included. A maximum length of 3,500 words is suggested. Please send no more than one prose work and no more than four poems. Successful contributors will be paid at the rate of £20 per published page.

ASLS
Department of Scottish Literature
7 University Gardens
University of Glasgow
Glasgow G12 8QH, Scotland

Tel +44 (0)141 330 5309
www.asls.org.uk

Jean Atkin

GALLOWARD

Galloward grips its hollow below the ridge;
stall and hall bared to the wind,
and gables crazed by rain.
I walk twisted, cagoule
squall-rattled in my ear.

Never cut down a holly. It streams
water past dry shade, protects
from wind and witches.
I climb a gate running in rust,
wade nettles among the tattered steadings.

The front door lies prone in the yard,
sneck latched to mud, and finger weathered.
I cross the threshold to a foundered house,
where slates grate under my step.
Voices called here, up the splintered stair.

I stand on the smoothed swag
of a flagstone. A window frame swings, emptied.
Out there a plough horse shifted its weight,
while a man ate his piece in the warm. Some woman
chose these flowery kitchen tiles.

Ribby with laths and flaking limewash,
Galloward is holding on,
but soaked, walls frail as paper.
By the hearth its lingering folk
mere smears of damp in a mushroom season.

GALLOWARD, 1925

A country boy's job,
the laying out of corpses
on a winter's day.

He treads the brae upward
each snow creak step
one nearer to the dead, and evening.

His landscape is re-written
in white, the dykes smoothed over,
so distances deceive.

Just now the holly keeps him right.
Higher up he sees
the oil lamp in the window –

for him, Galloward's grim
first footer, and the peat reek
reels him in.

He kicks off snow at the threshold.
The old wife lights a candle
and puts him to the stair.

The flame's waver hunchbacks him
on uneven walls. His heart pumping,
hot breath clouding the still room.

The old man, gape-mouthed,
in the cold bed, his eyes jellied wide.
His sharp tongue is shrunken,

and all his hardness
waxed away. Later, the boy will tell
how his own palms sweated.

Next day, he helps to heft
the coffin to the hearse. The old wife
shuts the door.

In keening snow they take him
to the kirkyard, snow so bad, that years on,
all the boy keeps

is how he hid from the gale,
and shambled drifts in the lee
of warm plumed horses.

Colin Begg

OBSERVATION POST
*(or: how I learned to stop denying and hate
that The Bomb remains)*

by a backroad in Cowal
beyond the powder mill,
an old bunker is padlocked
rusty water-filled,
above the village and the loch
high on a rush-flecked hill

louvred ventilators, green pipes
and grass-clogged filters:
instruments built to record
the would-be fallout spill from
mushrooms' (pouring over Gareloch,
over Coulport) cloudy gills

sporing over Holy Loch's
long-gone Americans, already death-dealing depth
in submarines filled from the pier
that my great-grandfather kept –

and I think how my father, in Glasgow
the night of Kennedy v. Khrushchev
talks of taking the last train home
to his village upwind and upstream
from city bars where friends waited
or silent watchers wept

and I think of my nightly childhood fear
of annihilation in my dreams
but those pesky Russians loved their kids
and now they're on our team.

From a backroad in Cowal
it seems nothing bears us ill,
we have no use of this old bunker
but satellites keep the drill,
mutually assured destruction lives
the old doctrine's with us still;

above the village and the loch
I can see the distant hill,
where there is a rocky honeycomb
of drones primed for the kill,
and down below in the glassy Kyles
the sonar pings sound shrill.

Kate Blackadder

HATTIE

It's a brown eggthing. A kiwi fruit it's for you Grandad, she says. I don't want it. Yes you do. I've halved it for you Grandad you can eat it with a spoon. I'm not your Grandad I say, me and my Hattie we never had children. She takes no notice. See, there you go, it's hard but you've a spoon. What a palaver, just for you. Doctor said you had to have vitamin see. Kiwi I say that's a bird not a fruit. From New Zealand it's a bird. Well maybe it is she says but you eat it up Grandad it's good for you. I'm not your Grandad I say. If you were my granddaughter you'd be a little redhead like my Hattie. You'd be beautiful like my Hattie. Not ugly. She takes no notice. She moves to the next bed. What's this Grandad? she says to the man, not feeling like your lunch today? She leaves me with this kiwi bird fruit hard, hard as stone. Green speckled black, a mossy stone. My Hattie's eyes. I can't eat my Hattie's eyes. I put them down, down under the sheet. Later she comes back wags her finger. You're not supposed to eat the skin Grandad. I'm not your Grandad I couldn't eat Hattie's eyes I say and she wags her finger. We'll have to give you more of your medicine if you talk like that Grandad. I turn my head away.

*

Behind the counter at the baker's I went dinner time. Hot meat pie. A Monday a new girl a white apron a white cap red hair. I said nothing bar asking for a hot meat pie. Afternoon I went for an Eccles cake then a cream puff. Closing time I was waiting, still in my overalls. What is it this time a French fancy said she smart as anything but there's a little smile so I said you're new and she said the baker's my Uncle Jack I've come up from the country I've just left school this will do till I find something better. What I said, what. She threw back her hair and I saw those eyes green moss emeralds even. What's your name. Alf. What's yours. Harriet you can call me Hattie. Hattie. My Hattie. I want the world she said. I want to give you the world Hattie I said but not to her not then. There's a big world out there Alf. I have plans she said. America maybe. I'll be in for my meat pie tomorrow I said. I'm painting a house round the corner. I'll save you the biggest one Hattie said. Jack's my uncle. He makes good meat pies. He's got a right beautiful niece I said and watched the blush rise. See you tomorrow Hattie. See you tomorrow Alf.

*

I sit in my chair. She pulls back the bedclothes. What's this, she shouts. She pushes me. You disgusting old man. The door opens. The other one comes in. Sharon, what on earth is going on? If I hear you speaking to Alf like that again I'll report you. You go and see to Bill. I'll tidy up here. I'm sorry you didn't like your kiwi fruit Alf, I thought it would be a change for you. Maybe you'd like an orange tomorrow.

*

He's having one of his better days, she says. As if I've been ill. Aren't you, Alf love? Alf love is it, I say, not Grandad today. She ignores that. Here's your daughter and your son-in-law come to see you. Look, they've brought you some nice flowers. I can see that I say you don't have to tell me. Although not nice, never liked chrysanths. Peter's not stopping Christine says, just dropped me off. I'm sorry Peter's not stopping. I like Peter. Peter claps me on the shoulder. See you soon. Right away Christine starts now Dad Sharon says you've been getting up in the night disturbing the others. Maybe Bill in the next bed, not me I say. I want to come home. Sharon doesn't like me.

Nonsense, says Christine, Sharon's very nice Look Dad I've brought you some biscuits fruit shortcake your favourite. Are they I say. She opens the packet puts two on a saucer. Here you are Dad. They are my favourite. She lays out two more then puts the packet in a plastic bag elastic round. I'll give it to Sharon ask her to give you some tomorrow she says. Not to that Sharon I'll never see them again like those chocolates. Nonsense, says Christine, she said you ate all the chocolates. I never I say, I never did. Oh Dad says Christine. She puts her hand in mine. I hold on. Christine's a good girl I say. Christine's a good little girl.

Oh Dad, says Christine and she holds on tight. Do you remember Dad when you and me and Mum had a holiday on that farm and you said you didn't like the cows and could I hold your hand until we were past them? I do remember, I say, but I don't. It's nice Christine holding my hand. I shut my eyes trying to remember. Are you sleepy Dad Christine says I should go. Don't go I say. She sits holding my hand.

I thought little Christine might be frightened of the cows, I say. I open my eyes. Christine is smiling. I know that now Dad she says. I know that now. That was a lovely holiday. There was a cat with six new kittens. Mum and I wanted to take one home but they were too young. And do you remember Mum fell asleep in the garden and got sunburn. Where is Mum? Why didn't Mum

come with you? Christine stops smiling. Oh Dad, she says you
know Mum's gone. Dead. Twenty years ago. Dead! No, not dead I
say. Yes says Christine. I didn't know that. You didn't tell me. Why
didn't you tell me. Oh Dad, says Christine. I must be going get the
bus. Peter's supper. We're going to the cinema. She kisses the top of
my head. I'll see you Saturday.

Can I come home with you and Peter. Not today Christine
says, not today Dad. Maybe on your birthday. Christine I call,
Christine, but she's away. Dead I say nobody told me. What? says
that Sharon person. You're not dead Grandad not yet. Half dead
maybe. She laughs. I wasn't frightened of the cows I say to Bill
Trent when we pass his bed. Good man says Bill. Good man, good
man, good man.

*

*I want to kiss you Hattie. Do you Alf. Yes I do. Come round here said
Hattie Uncle Jack's out. You have green eyes. I know I do Alf. Hattie
giggled. You have beautiful eyes Hattie. And beautiful lips. Hattie let
me kiss her. You do say nice things Alf say some more. You're lovely
Hattie lovely lovely. I'm working hard Hattie, saving up. Are you Alf,
what for. For a nice house Hattie for a home. Let's go to the pictures
Alf I like Clark Gable. I like you Hattie, I like you.*

*

Alf love here's Christine, here's your daughter to see you. I don't
have a daughter. Yes you do. She nips above the elbow. Don't nip
me. There's a plump woman wearing a yellow jumper. Oh Dad
says Yellow Jumper, no one's nipping you. Thank you Sharon.
Dad, look I've brought you some biscuits. Fruit shortcake, your
favourite. Oh Dad, don't, don't do that. What a mess. Colin drove
me over. Remember I told you he passed his test last week. He's
parking the car, oh here he is now. Colin I'm just going to go and
get a brush. Gramps dropped the biscuits and stood on them. You
stay here with him.

OK, hi Gramps. Who's Gramps. You're Gramps says the boy,
you're my Gramps. I'm not, I'm not. OK mate, says the boy, no
problem. What's that in your ear. A stud. Isn't it cool. Your hair's
too long for the army. That's all right mate, I'm at college. Did
Mum tell you I'd passed my driving test. Can I come home with
you in your car. I don't think so Gramps, not today, Mum said
maybe on your birthday. Who's Gramps. Tell you what mate, one
day I'll take you out in the car. Mum doesn't need to know. How
about that. We'll go for a drive in the country.

Colin what are you saying. You know the last time we took him in the car he tried to get out on the motorway. Oh Mum didn't see you. Poor old Gramps what a life stuck in here. Smells of pee and mashed potato. He's going to have to be moved Colin. He's wandering in the night Sharon says. He'll have to move somewhere more secure. Poor old Gramps. We had some good times before he turned funny didn't we. He used to come and watch me play football. He liked a game of draughts and dominoes. He told me stories about the war, playing in the military band and all that. And remember when he painted my bedroom red and white striped. I know Colin thank God your grandma isn't here to see him now. I'm just going to have a word with the Matron. Stay here with him Colin.

The boy picks up a paper. Look Gramps, look mate, there's a bit here about the Grand Prix. It was on television yesterday. He sits beside me and shows me pictures. I lean against him. Where's my Hattie. Don't know mate he says, were you wearing one. Oh Mum he says, Gramps wants his hat. What hat says Yellow Jumper. He doesn't need a hat. Although he used to wear a cap all the time. Do you remember. A tweed cap.

*

Sunday, Hattie, would you like to come cycling in the country. We could stop somewhere for tea. Day out in the country. Borrow a bike for you. Oh no Alf. No. I don't like the country, it's boring. But I thought Hattie we could see your family, I'd like to see your family in the country. What for. Not this Sunday Alf. Let's go to the pictures Alf, I like Errol Flynn. I thought you liked Clark Gable Hattie. I did but now I like Errol Flynn. Or we could go dancing. Can we go dancing Alf. What about next Sunday to the country? I don't know Alf I don't know the country's dull I don't like cycling no Alf I don't want to. I could borrow a car maybe. My chum's got a car I'll ask. Oh Alf. Oh Alf. Oh yes I'll wear my new dress. You'll love it Alf. I love you Hattie. Do you Alf.

*

It's the other one. She says Alf your family is here for your birthday. Christine and Peter and Colin are all here. I'm going home on my birthday. I don't think so Alf she says, they've brought you a lovely cake with a candle and presents. Come down to the lounge she says. We'll have a bit of a party. That will be nice won't it? Cheer you up. Oh Dad says Christine whatever have you done to your hand, your arm. She says, I thought someone had phoned to tell

you, Mrs Watson. Alf burnt himself two nights ago. When he was
having a bath. He turned on the hot tap when Sharon's back was
turned. I never I say, I never did. I thought someone had phoned,
she says, I'm so sorry. We called the doctor. He's had painkillers.
Now Alf what do you think of that lovely cake. It's a lovely birthday
cake Alf. That car boy is here. I've brought you a present Gramps
he says. I've brought you a cap. He puts it on my head. I pull it off.
Look Gramps he says it's a good cap, it's a Man. United cap. He
puts it back on. I'll blow out your candle for you he says. Will you
manage the cake with your hand Dad says Christine. I'll cut you a
piece of birthday cake Dad. I want to come home with you. Can I
come home on my birthday. I'm sorry Dad. Not today. Maybe at
Christmas-time. Oh Peter we must remember to get a Christmas
present for Sharon. She's been so good to Dad. Oh, don't do that.
If you don't want it Dad I've got some Eccles cakes as well, you
used to like those.

*

*here's your cake Alf I'm leaving Uncle Jack's it's boring I want some fun
I want to see the world my face is my fortune he said a man said a big
man in a camel hair coat*
HATTIE
Dad, please. Don't shout.
*came Uncle Jack's ask directions your face is your fortune I'm leaving
sorry you're upset Alf I never said I loved you I never I never did I
never did*
Dad, please. Calm down. Who is Hattie?
Was Hattie my grandma's name?
No no her name was Ellen. Dad, don't cry. Peter have you got
a hankie.
Where's Hattie. Hattie come back.
a big man in a camel hair coat
Who's Hattie. Who is this Hattie, Dad.
HATTIE
Please calm down. Peter, go and get Sharon. Dad. Please. Oh,
Sharon. Dad's ever so upset.
Now Alf, what's the problem. You've got presents. And a lovely
birthday cake.
I'm going home on my birthday. Home.
That's right Alf love. That's right. You come with me. I'll look
after him, Mrs Watson.
Don't you worry.

Isobel Boyle

MWANIKI

He's dead I know but
I can hear his bass voice shout 'bafu, bafu!' and
feel the slap slap of his splayed brown feet,
cracked at the heels, chasing behind me.
I fall into his arms in a breathless mass of laughter.

Childishly bored
I seek him out in the dark back kitchen
where I am not supposed to be but
he won't tell.
I watch the potato peelings fall
from between his pink-palmed hands
and smell the hiss of his spit as he tests the flat iron.
He lets me pattern the pie with a fork
and smooth my father's handkerchiefs.
On an upturned bucket
he lets me dry the knives
under his sharp gaze.
He won't tell.

He's dead I know and it's long ago but
the deep, dark smell of him
rising from my polished chestnut table
and the sound of the catch of his rough hands on my jersey
as he let me go
are with me here.

(*Bafu* – Kiswahili for bath)

David Cameron

THE SILENT

The distance between my house in Blackbraes and Marie Connolly's house in Glen Doll was a mile and a half: a long walk for short legs. But I had to stop off at Alison Lea and pick up my friend Stephen first. Glen Doll, Alison Lea: erotic names. As though a street could be a huge recumbent girl; Alice on her back after finishing off the cake labelled EAT ME.

Stephen kept me waiting downstairs while his mum moved from room to room. I was worried that she would frustrate our plans, send Stephen for a message or ask me at length about my own mum.

'I'm dead excited, Rooney Roots,' I said as we made it outside.

'I'm dead excited too, Cammy,' Stephen said.

We could have taken the path that skirted the wilderness known as The Silent. Instead we cut through Hunter, where Protestant boys threw stones at passing Catholic boys like us. So we were told. On this July evening the school grounds were happily empty of other children. Only the huge metal bins stood guard.

We were out of Calderwood, into the newer conurbation of St Leonards. Clumps of trees here were Scandinavian in their neatness, the earth under them dusty and flat. Tall wooden fences backed onto white houses, but the gardens were visible through the slats, not walled in like the gardens at home.

'Do you remember the first time we came down here?' Stephen asked.

'No.'

'You must remember. You brought a bright orange ball that had a thorn still stuck in it.'

'I remember the ball. Were we meeting the girls?'

'Not that time. Just Caffy and Cakes. We played a five-elevener with them. I can't believe you don't remember.'

'Who won?'

'Them, I think.'

We came to a large open square where people our age and younger congregated. It was here, a stone's throw from Glen Doll, that we were to meet the two girls. My mouth was dry already.

'Have we time to go to the shop?'

'What for?'

'A bottle of Irn-Bru.'

'I don't think so.'

We stood with thumbs hooked into our pockets, watching the downhill wheelies of daredevils on Chopper bikes. We must have stood like that for a full ten minutes. At one point I caught Stephen's eye just after we'd been staring in the same direction – over towards Glyn McGlynn's house. We knew he'd be home. Glyn was always home. Or if his mum let him outside, it was only ever to the patch of ground immediately in front of the house.

Stephen was shouting in my ear. 'Caffy! Cakes!'

Here they were again, Paul McCafferty and Kevin Cairns, with a football even, traipsing over from the direction of the swing park. I felt my spirit sag. Tonight was meant to be an amorous rendezvous, not a kick about. What would Marie say?

*

Well, I would find out. Through the trees we saw the two girls approach, so close to each other that they might have been sewn together. Marie was dressed in jeans and a white, wide-sleeved top that didn't drain any of the blondeness from her hair, Cheryl in a short brown dress with a dark slender belt around the waist.

'Hello, David,' Marie said. 'Stephen, Kevin, Paul.'

The ball immediately got kicked between us boys, till it landed at Cheryl's sandalled feet. She kicked it straight in front of her with force.

'Snap,' Marie whispered, looking me up and down. 'Our clothes,' she said. I hadn't registered that we were both in blue and white.

'He's blushing,' Cheryl said, directing all eyes at me. 'He's blushing, he's blushing, he's blushing.'

Stephen, back with the ball, said: 'That's nothing. Have you seen the state of my neck? Burnt to a frazzle. Don't touch it but.'

Kevin made slapstick efforts to get at Stephen's neck. Nobody laughed, so he took the ball instead and bounced it hard. I watched him after that – it helped my cheeks cool to watch him. I saw that, as the talk flashed round, he would bounce the ball rather than speak. I could see in his face when a thought formed, and then he would bounce the ball again, until the thought disappeared again.

'Every hour, every minute, seemed to last eternally,' the girls sang. They were standing side-on to each other, Cheryl's arm on Marie's shoulder. 'I was so afraid, Fernando …'

'Who's this?' Stephen asked, taking a step back before grinning and pulling up his shoulders.

'Ted Heath. Too easy, do another one.'

'OK, who's this?'

'Captain Mainwaring.'

'Nope.'

'Sergeant Bilko.'

'Nope.'

'Ted Heath again.'

'No!'

'Hello, guys. Who's the comedian?'

I wanted to say 'Impressionist' as the man stepped into the circle we'd formed. The look of alarm on Kevin's face spread round us all.

'Relax, everyone,' the man said. 'I only want to chew the fat with you. Are you all from around here?'

'Us four are, not those two,' Marie said.

'Where you from, boys?'

'Calderwood,' Stephen said.

'You look like Calderwood boys. They grow them short up there. I'm a West Mains man.'

'What are you doing here?' Marie asked.

'Visiting a pal, but he's not in. Now I'm just chewing the fat with you guys. Anybody want a Polo?'

He very carefully took a packet of Polo Mints from his jeans.

'Shrink-to-fit, these. I stayed in the bath a bit too long but. Here, have a Polo. It's a great wee mint, isn't it? Stroke of genius having a hole in the middle. Think how much mint they're saving, then they charge full whack for something that's basically hollow.'

'I've heard that said before,' Marie said.

'You heard it before because it's true. Have one, why don't you.'

'No thanks. I don't accept sweeties from strangers.'

We all laughed.

'It gave this town its nickname, did you know *that*? Polo Mint City, on account of the fact it's got so many roundabouts. Did you not know that? You Calderwood boys'll be familiar with the Whirlies. That roundabout's murder. Women drivers shouldn't be let on it, they've no lane discipline. No offence, darlings.'

'Can you drive?' Marie asked, serenely.

'Got my Provisional. Once I get me a nice wee motor, it'll be bye-bye Polo Mint City. Just you watch me.'

We were all watching him, intently. There was an awkward moment while he looked back at us, sizing up the situation.

'Right, I'm going to show you something very special now. Just got to roll up my sleeves first.'

He unbuttoned the cuffs of his shirt and folded them neatly back on themselves, again and again, as far up as the denim would fold.

'Now look at these beauties.'

He flexed his upper-arm muscles and said: 'Touch them. Go on. They're rock-hard. And that's only the biceps. Wait till you see my pectorals.'

He unbuttoned his shirt fully.

'I don't believe this is happening,' Marie said, as Cheryl screamed girlishly.

'The thing about the human body is, all the muscles and sinews are interconnected. If I tense these muscles here, watch what happens to my stomach. You can punch my stomach now, as hard as you want. Go on, punch it hard.'

We lined up to punch the talkative stranger, first Paul, then Stephen, then Kevin, then me. I kept my fist clenched till it was my turn.

'Wouldn't you know it? Little sailor boy packs the strongest punch,' he said. 'Always the quiet ones you've got to watch.'

'Let me have a go,' Marie said.

'Don't!' Cheryl said.

'Can't do it,' the man said, to my relief. 'It wouldn't be right. Now, boys, I'm going to let you into a secret you'll remember the rest of your lives. What did I do to deserve muscles as rock-hard as these? Two-minute exercises: that's all. You put your fingers like this ...'

He locked his hands together so that they resembled one of those S-clasp buckles we'd grown out of; then pulled, counting to ten; reversed hands and repeated.

'Never do it for more than two minutes at a time,' he said.

We watched in awe before trying it out for ourselves. He cut an impressive figure there, standing on the hillock stripped to the waist with his blow-dried hair down to his shoulders and hands clasped in front of his chest. And it was true: the exercise produced Samson-like powers in us for seconds afterwards.

'Do you know this one?' Paul asked, his face shining up at the man. Next Paul arranged Kevin cross-legged and had the three of us try to lift him then press our palms down hard on his head and try to lift him again using only our index and middle fingers.

'What you've done there is tighten your biceps to make it easier for you to lift your friend.'

'I knew that,' Paul said, crestfallen. 'I just wanted to show you.'

One of the Chopper boys screeched to a halt beside us. 'Veronica's going mental again,' he shouted across the square.

*

First the boys on their bikes, then a crowd from the swing park, streamed past. Marie had a pained look on her face, but Cheryl tugged at her sleeve, and the momentum of the moment caused us all to drift towards the source of excitement. I glanced back at the man: he seemed, if anything, to be smiling.

I tried to keep close to Marie in case she would reach for my hand, as she occasionally, miraculously did in the dark of the school's TV room.

The commotion was happening outside a glass-fronted block of flats. Here the crowd swelled and then stopped, exposing a distraught girl on the lawn.

'I fucking hate you, fucking cunt,' she shouted up at a window – it wasn't clear which one. 'You fucking spastic, I wish you were fucking dead, you cunting fuck.'

'Veronica! Veronica! Over here, Veronica!'

'Shut the fuck up, spasmo,' she snapped back at a bystander, a boy.

'She's epileptic,' Stephen said beside me. I looked at him. Cheryl was standing there too, Kevin further back, next to Paul. I couldn't see Marie.

'Did she burn your tea, Veronica?'

She? I looked up at the windows again. Sure enough, the figure of a woman, barely visible through the shimmering, green reflection of the trees, moved across a pane.

'Fucking bitch. Fucking *bitch*.'

A man in a bunnet passed by, carrying two slender bags of shopping, and saying: 'Did you ever hear the like?'

I was exhilarated. Here was a girl heroically screaming words we longed to scream at our own mothers too sometimes. Because I understood: the woman who appeared only to disappear again was this mad girl's mother. Why didn't she come downstairs and lead her daughter inside? I didn't want her to. Not yet. I had heard all the swear words before, but not at once or delivered so vehemently. We moved back as Veronica lunged towards us, and crept forward as she aimed her rage at the window. I liked it best when she raged, when her features matched the violence of her words. But then a haunted, panicked look would take over: a look of extreme, fleeting remorse. It was like nothing I had witnessed before. The sheer repetition, the alternation between long rage and short remorse, began to make her seem comfortingly mechanical, like a doll, a clockwork doll. Still, I cowed whenever her eyes swept over mine. What if our eyes locked and she perceived something in me? What was that something? What if she shouted it to the crowd?

'Get down here, bitch. Cunting bitch.'

When I turned round again, not even Stephen was there. I couldn't tell how many minutes had passed. Surely a grown-up would come and put a stop to it. Somebody must have called the police by now. The police were sure to arrive.

Giles Conisbee

PEAT

She said, I want you to write, write about it
she said, about the air, the smell of it.

So I sat down to write about the smell of peat
but all I got was the gentle bite of grazing sheep,
moving thin away on the hillside and frayed trawler
rope looped over gates with seaman knots, rocks
out-strung from ná Geárrannan roofs like unpicked fruit
or flowers in the straw-coloured hair of a girl
and the June sea-mist hugging I don't know what.
And came to my mind the sky, bare for the lack
of trees and sea-gifts washed up, used everywhere.

I want to read about it she said, about the air,
the smell of it. Write about it, she said.

So I sat down to write about the smell of peat
but all I got was muffled waves of stagnant
seaweed hoarded to the shore by weak tides
and set upon by millions of sand flies,
and light smooth grey boulders that break the line
between sea and sand like tumbled memories,
a grind of rock and shell, lap and suck and the odd bird
kiting overhead. And came to my mind the Islanders' love
of cut pipes for post boxes and weavers running to a standstill.

She said write about it, the smell of the peat, the burning
of the years in the air. I want you to write about it, she said.

So I sat down to write on a manmade bench,
a sort of perfect perch where reflections could take shape
but all I got was the careful crunch of tourist feet
on the gravel paths between blackhouse runs,
and camera ignition bleeps, fake shutter snaps,
sounds made to fool you into thinking what you feel is real,
solid and old when it's clearly not, it's shiny-thin
digital new and everything is disposable, except for here,
in this place, where nothing goes to waste.

She said I want you to write about it, the smell of the peat,
the wild flower scent held still for lifetimes, now released.
Write about it she said, I want you to.

So I sat down to write about the smell of peat
but all I got was carrot cake and coffee, soup of the day
and grubby urges, sunglasses in the museum shop,
cards on sale and all things, everything, made in Harris Tweed.
And it came to mind that the smell of peat is a longing,
glimmering in the bracken, melancholy in bog, alone
and nooked like hillside heathers and sheep, rugged
and chilled, struggled like old rope, persistent as the tides,
laid out syrup-dark and smooth on a pallet to dry.

Catherine Czerkawska

A QUIET AFTERNOON IN THE MUSEUM OF TORTURE

'Davy. Come and look at this.'

Her husband is loitering in another room, reading graphic descriptions of cruelty. Ros turns her attention back to the photograph of a real woman, naked, except for the spiked metal contraption which doesn't seem to be troubling her at all. The woman stands there, plump and complacent, hands by her sides. It's an old photograph, from the 1920s perhaps. She has long hair, a pretty face, a round belly. Ros wonders about the picture. Was it from a serious medical text or, more likely, one of those naughty postcards that gentlemen used to pass around for their private titillation? She remembers reading that most of the girls in those pictures were ruthlessly exploited by the photographers but this woman looks faintly bored if anything. Ros reads the caption.

'The chastity belt had very little to do with knights locking away their wives while they went off on Crusades. It was much more about women defending themselves against rape, during times of siege or on dangerous journeys.'

Unlike the other exhibits, at least the chastity belt seems to have had a reasonable purpose. As for the rest – a miscellany of cruelty – how could so much ingenuity be dedicated to such dreadful ends? And why are so many of these things decorated? Why the intricate carving, the brilliant colours? Why go the length of making them so *pretty*?

She can hear her husband's footsteps, the characteristic jiggle of coins and keys in his pocket, but otherwise the museum is quiet. He comes up behind her and puts his hands on her shoulders while he looks at the chastity belt, with its curved, outward-facing spikes.

'Ouch,' he says. 'That would set your gas at a peep, wouldn't it?' He peers more closely. 'Christ you wouldn't even want to have a wee feel, would you?'

'I think that's the general idea.'

*

It is an October afternoon in this small hill town in Tuscany. And it is raining. They were on their way to seek shelter in the Etruscan Museum when Davy was sidetracked by the sign advertising the *Museo Della Tortura* with a wooden cage containing a skeleton in the doorway.

'Oh wow,' he said. 'Come on. Let's go in.'

'But the baby …'

'The baby's fast asleep. He won't know where he is. His world is one giant milk bar.'

It's true enough. Angus is asleep in his sling, his cheek turned towards her breast. He is too heavy for it now, a big boy, gaining weight fast, and her back hurts but he seems so comfortable that she puts up with it for the sake of peace and quiet.

This is their first holiday as a family. Until now, it has always been just the two of them, exploring foreign cities, eating, drinking a bit too much wine, making love, making – as it turned out – a baby. Now, just getting away from home together seems like an achievement. She is tired all the time. She has to be careful what she eats because some foods upset the baby. And as for lovemaking … she finds herself thinking of the chastity belt with approval.

'Don't you think he's a bit young for flying?' said her mother. But she put the baby discreetly to the breast for most of the journey. He suckled and slept, alternately. When they were getting off the plane, a woman peered over her shoulder.

'My God, such a new baby. How did you keep him so quiet?'

I just plugged him in, she thought, but instead she said, 'He's a good baby. A good boy.'

*

They have rented a small farmhouse on the edge of a hill village. Davy drives the hire car warily from Pisa along roads that are neither straight nor level, but elbow their way up and down hills at alarming angles.

'Well the Romans sure didn't build these.'

'Maybe it was the local boys.'

Davy grins. 'Do you smell burning clutch?'

She navigates, while the baby sleeps, securely strapped in behind them. Ponsacco, La Streza, Laiatico. She checks off a litany of names, her finger on the map, tracing the bendy roads and the unfamiliar syllables.

'Do you know that Andrea Boccelli comes from La Streza?'

Davy shakes his head. 'Not a lot of people know that.'

The day is damp, the leaves beginning to tumble around them. All the colours are clear and deep. The light gets into her head and stays there. Back in Scotland, everything will seem subdued and subtle for weeks. The narrow road climbs through the village, between red-roofed houses, until they are almost out the other side, among the trees again. From the terrace of the villa they can see a hundred villages and towns and houses like this one, clinging to the tops of hills, above layers of landscape, with creamy clouds sandwiched between.

The villa is clean with white painted walls and shiny terracotta floors. Thank God, she thinks, with the baby on her mind. There is a playroom with toys, the kitchen cupboards have olive oil, balsamic vinegar, packets of pasta, left by previous occupants. The bathroom has shampoo and shower gel and a large centipede who lives behind the gas boiler and ventures out infrequently to inspect the visitors.

The place is festooned with handwritten notes from the housekeeper.

'When you return to your house, you leave rubbish in the house because cats make a hole in bags.'

'No deliver this key to any place.'

'This is a kit of first aid when necessary.'

There are bookshelves stuffed with novels in bright covers, books with titles in which words like sun, summer, lemons, and the inevitable Tuscany, figure prominently. She flicks through them, nursing the baby, a cooling cup of tea at her side, while Davy prowls about, investigating. She notes that the stories are invariably about somebody buying a dilapidated Tuscan farmhouse, and renovating it, with the help or hindrance of eccentric but kindly natives. The protagonists drink local wine, eat local fruit and vegetables, marvelling at their cheapness, sometimes fall in love (but almost never, she notices, with the locals), meet with disaster, overcome all their tribulations and live happily ever after.

Later in the week she will discover the other kind of book about Italy tucked away on these same shelves: stories of bureaucracy and corruption, cautionary tales from those self-consciously in the know. She finds that she likes them even less, if anything, than the honest-to-God fantasies.

'Plenty to read,' observes Davy.

She shrugs. 'You reckon?'

She has brought her own reading matter, a bleak Scottish detective novel. She feels herself resisting the pull of the place, confused by its glamour and its outlandishness.

There is a shop down in the village with ten kinds of cheese, as many varieties of salami and pasta, tins of tomatoes and anchovies, and packets of Lavazzo coffee as well as shelves full of cleaning materials. There is a freezer cabinet, and fresh bread, but little in the way of fruit or vegetables.

'Perhaps people grow those themselves,' says Davy.

'Perhaps they buy them in the supermarket in the next town.'
She can't seem to stop herself from making these snappy
rejoinders. Davy doesn't reply, unwilling to get into an argument.
Hormones, he thinks. Hormones, she thinks too. But she feels the
need to resist something. The place is too easy. She can't fathom
it at all.

'*Buongiorno*,' say the locals, meeting them on the road down
to the shop, smiling at the baby.

In the garden of the villa there is a fig tree, but although the figs
are soft and ripe, there are holes in them where insects have bored
deep inside. The rosemary is in bright blue bloom all over again.
There are pots of thyme, and pomegranate trees, shrub sized, with
a few fruits still clinging to their branches. She is faintly disturbed
by the way in which each fruit opens out, the skin stretching like
a purple mouth so that the drying seeds can fall to the ground
beneath.

After supper, they sit on the terrace and drink wine until the
light leaches out of the sky and a thousand lamps are strung out
across the hills with dark valleys between. No-one lives in the
valleys and the roads don't go there. They are dangerous pools of
darkness between the hilltop illuminations.

'Do you know,' says Davy, who has been reading one of the
cautionary tales, 'that the Italians consider it uncouth to carry on
drinking wine after you have stopped eating? You can drink other
things, *grappa* for instance, but not wine.'

'Not a lot of people know that,' she says.

The bed is large and comfortable, and there is a cot for the
baby which they place beside it. He wakes in the night for milk,
and she wraps him in a shawl and takes him onto the terrace so
as not to wake Davy. It is still warm out there and she sits on one
of the plastic chairs. The silence, above and beyond the sucking
noises of the baby's lips against her breast, is absolute. The air is
fresh, with a faint undertone of sulphur. When she mentioned it
to Davy, last night, he laughed at her.

'You and your smells,' he told her. 'I think it's just wood
smoke.'

But sitting out here, she is aware of it again, just the faintest
whiff of hell. She cups the baby's head in her hand defensively and
changes sides.

*

In the morning they are woken by the sound of huntsmen in the
woods beyond the house.

'Christ,' says Davy. 'That's a rifle, not a shotgun.'

'What are they shooting?'

'I don't know. Birds. Rabbits. Could be wild boar I suppose.'

Later that day, they find a signboard down in the village pointing the way to a *mofeta* which seems, from the illustration, to be some kind of volcanic emission.

'I told you so.'

'What did you tell me?'

'Sulphur. I could smell it again in the night.'

About half a mile from the village, they find another signpost, and following a rocky track between shrubs, they come across a gully where a small eruption fulminates with ash and with mud that seems to have a life of its own, bubbling and heaving in sinister fashion. There is a pool of water next to it, at what cookery books call a 'rolling boil'. The signs warn that it will be *pericoloso* to go any closer because of the concentrations of CO_2 in the air.

'I wonder what the English for *mofeta* is?'

'Fumarole,' she says, dredging the word up from somewhere.

'Aren't you the smart one?' says Davy.

The trees are all tagged and there is obviously some kind of scientific experiment in process. Davy wants to stay and watch the mud, but she is seized with fear for the baby, and heads back up the track again, not willing to wait for him. Halfway up, a big brindled dog bursts from the undergrowth. She halts but it is a friendly creature, cavorting around her briefly, before elbowing her aside and heading on up the track. The baby, lulled by the motion of her walking, sleeps. It has just started to rain, so when she has put some distance between herself and the fumarole, she shelters beneath the low trees to wait for Davy. The pungent scent of mint envelops her, rising from beneath her feet. As soon as she stops moving, the baby wakes up and wrinkles his nose. Perhaps he can smell the mint too, or perhaps he is only hungry.

'Not now,' she whispers to him. 'You'll have to wait till we get back to the house.'

He gazes up at her with blue, unfocused eyes and then dozes again.

She hears the snapping of twigs as somebody pushes through the undergrowth. The dog comes rushing back down the path to greet the newcomer. She is expecting to see Davy, but instead, an elderly man strides out of the trees. She has an impression of a blue waterproof stretched over a bulging stomach, the gun slung over his back, pink cheeks, raindrops on grey hair. He nods to her, unsmiling, and then he is gone, the dog frisking around him. She wonders if they have ruined his day's hunting with their noise but the dog wasn't exactly subtle either.

Davy is picking his way up the track.

'Still asleep?' he asks.

'Seems to be.'

'We'll pay for it tonight,' he says, Scottish to the bone.

*

That was yesterday. But today they are in the Museum of Torture. They are the only visitors on this quiet afternoon, and she is gazing at an old wooden rocking horse. What is a rocking horse doing in such a place, she wonders? They have already talked about getting one for Angus. They have seen pictures in glossy magazines, sent for brochures, wondered if they will be able to afford one before their son is too big to ride it.

'It's you that wants one, really,' says Davy, and she can't deny it.

This horse is in dark wood with savage teeth and a leather saddle. Bewildered, she reads the caption. 'This rocking horse was bought by a nobleman for his son. But the six-year-old child became too fond of the horse, and neglected his studies so that he could ride on it. The father asked a local craftsman to alter the saddle, so that riding the horse became a punishment rather than a pleasure.'

She looks more closely at the saddle and sees that somebody has fashioned it into peaks and cones of hard leather. She feels breathless, stifled, as though she can't get enough air into her lungs. She turns away, heading for the exit.

The baby, aware of her distress, stirs and wails. Outside the museum, she sways from side to side, patting his back. The rain has stopped. An old woman, perched on a stone bench in the watery sunlight, smiles up at her, and indicates the seat beside her. She sits down briefly, but the bench smells of pee, so she gets up again, jiggling him, until Davy dawdles out of the museum.

'Are you all right?' he asks. 'I wondered where you'd gone.'

'I just got too hot in there. I needed some fresh air.'

'Don't think much to the horse, do you?'

'No.'

'Nasty idea. Imagine doing that.'

His composure angers her.

'Imagine,' she says.

The thought of Angus's peachy bottom in contact with those leather spikes sets her teeth on edge. Emotions clash and collide in her head. How could they? How could anybody?

They head back to the car, deciding to save the Etruscans for another day.

'You look very tired, Rosy Posy,' he says, suddenly solicitous.

He only calls her Rosy Posy when he is worried about her. She thinks she might be going to cry, and controls herself with an effort.

When they go back to Scotland, people will say 'What was it like? In Tuscany? Was it nice?'

'It wasn't what I expected.'

'What did you expect?'

'I think I sort of expected the Cotswolds with sunshine. All those Sunday supplements. You know?'

'And?'

'And it's nothing like that. It's much more savage. A much more savage place altogether.'

'Didn't you like it then?' her friends and relatives will say, disappointed.

'I loved it. It just wasn't what I expected. That's all.'

*

After the museum, they drive back to the house and later on, they walk down into the village for provisions. The houses there are dilapidated but orderly. She is lost in thoughts about the lives of these people, enmeshed in her own curiosity. She wants to open each neat front door and peer in. She tries to read the inhabitants from their possessions. She even finds herself examining the washing, strung out on lines from window to window, and across terraces: trousers, underwear, towels, a pillowcase with a print of a cat's face, a Mickey Mouse duvet cover.

When she sees an elderly woman buying pasta, cheese, pancetta and eggs, she imagines the meal, pictures a family eating together around a big table. Her own grandmother is dead; her parents separated and remarried other people long ago. Davy isn't close to his family either. She has a fleeting vision of herself running after this woman.

Take me with you, she thinks. Let me come home with you. Let me sit in your kitchen while you cook. Let me tell you what has happened to me. Comfort me with food. Feed me on pasta. Fill me with potatoes roasted with olive oil and rosemary. Bake me a chestnut cake and panna cotta with speckles of vanilla. Creamy panna cotta that slides down like mother's milk. Let me live in a book about your life, where I might feel safe.

The woman stretches out a wrinkled hand and pats the baby's head. '*Bellissimo!*' she says.

*

That night, the baby refuses to sleep. Colicky, he struggles, girns and moans, pulling his dimpled knees close to his chest. He wants to suckle, but her milk does nothing to comfort him. At last he falls asleep, sprawled on Davy's chest. Then they tuck him down between them in the bed. Her mother and her health visitor would frown at this, but she doesn't care. Some nights, it is the only way they can get any rest. He is a big boy, and though he always rolls onto his tummy in his cot, he invariably sleeps safely on his back when he is in bed with them, his breathing peacefully tuned to theirs. Even in sleep they are aware of his presence. He lies between them like a small oven, radiating warmth.

'I love the feel of him there,' says Davy, unexpectedly. 'Don't you, Ros?'

The latest childcare fad is something called 'controlled crying'.

'Mothers who learn to let their babies cry themselves to sleep have better nights and less postnatal depression,' said one report, pointed out to her by her GP. She irritates him by telling him that this seems so unscientific as to be meaningless. Maybe mothers who learn to let their babies cry are unfeeling. Maybe they didn't have postnatal depression – which is surely hormonal – in the first place. And what exactly do the researchers mean by 'better nights' since breastfed babies generally wake up for a feed or sometimes two? The doctor cannot answer any of these questions and retreats into disgruntled silence.

'That's my Ros,' says Davy when she tells him about it afterwards.

But one of Davy's colleagues at work is following the regime to the letter.

'It works,' he told Davy. 'My wife wasn't convinced at first, but I persuaded her, and it works. You should try it.'

'God's sake,' said Davy. 'They prosecute people for doing that.'

'For controlled crying?'

'For making young primates sleep alone in small cages. They call it animal cruelty.'

Davy can never hold his tongue either. It is one more thing that they have in common.

Now they lie in bed, in a villa in Tuscany, the three of them in a row.

She thinks, Roll over, roll over, so they all rolled over and one fell out ...

Terror assails her. What would he do without me? she thinks. What would they do, both of them, if anything happened to me?

Davy stirs, aware of her unease.

'Are you all right?'

'Yes. Just a bit panicky.'

'Slow your breathing.'

'I'm trying.'

She turns over and watches the baby in the half light from the hallway. Expressions flit across his face, experimental emotions, as though he is auditioning for the man he will become.

'Nobody told me,' she says, quietly.

'They told us it would change our lives. Everyone said that and we didn't believe them.'

'But they never told me it would hurt this much.'

All the antenatal care had been about choices. Birth plans. Breast is best. Not once had anyone mentioned this pain.

Davy grimaces. 'I seem to remember one friend of yours talking about shitting a melon.'

'I don't mean that.'

'You told me you'd forgotten about the pain as soon as he was born.'

'So I have.'

'Well I can't forget it. Seeing you like that. I thought I might lose you.'

'But nobody told us about *this* pain, did they?'

'What?' he says, really alarmed now. 'What pain?'

'Don't you feel it? Or is it only me? It can't only be me. I keep thinking of that bloody rocking horse.'

'I know. It was horrible.'

'It's as though I've lost some shield, some protective coating. I'm a hostage to my own imagination and it hurts!'

There are paedophiles, terrorists, earthquakes. Sometimes the news seems to be about nothing but distressed or dying children. Despair overwhelms her, several times a day. Even films and other fictions are unbearably poignant.

'Oh God!' she says. 'What will happen to him if I'm not here?'

'You're not going anywhere, are you?'

'No.'

'Well then.'

'But don't you see?' she tells him. 'It isn't just him.' She hesitates. 'It's every child. It's like being mother to the whole world.'

He lies there for a moment, looking at the ceiling. 'I know,' he says, unexpectedly. Just for a moment, she sees his face crumble into vulnerability. 'I do know. Father too. Father to the whole world as well.'

He props himself up on one elbow and kisses his son's cheek.

"This is a kit of first aid when necessary,' he says. 'Isn't it, Angus?'

The baby stirs and flexes his perfect fingers.

From outside comes the first crackle and echo of gunfire. The morning slaughter has begun.

John Duffy

A SLEEPING CROON

Coorie doon
  wee man
close your eyes
  in Cairnbaan
overhead
  the big moon
in your ear
  your mother croons
songs for sleep
  lullabies
coorie doon
  close your eyes
you will sleep
  very soon
cuddle up
  and coorie doon
on this narrow
  strip of land
Loch Sween
  Cairnbaan
from above
  moonshine
on the waters
  of Loch Fyne
on the shifty
  briny sea
on your grandma
  and on me
on the wriggling
  River Add
on the straight canal
  your dad
comes and works
  to keep in trim
all the boats
  depend on him
every star
  is a jewel
and you will sleep

                in Ullapool
        across the hills
                many miles
        sleeping near
                the Summer Isles
        herrings landed
                cran by cran
        Cairnbaan
                wee man
        wee man
                Cairnbaan
                        Cairnbaan
                                wee man
                                    Cairnbaan............

Rob Ewing

FIRST CONTACT

First: divine the waters. The fisherman
Scans the salt-scoured thrift, takes up a clump
And chews the pink bland tips and says:
We go *there,* this night.

There being twenty mile west of the Voe
To a place of sullen wind and torrid sea
Where the sinker drops past fifty fathom, a deep
Where salty rumoured MacLeods swoon eyeless

In the black. No anchorage here.
A net dropped, then a line as long as the highest
Stac. The sea a maw of gaping devil-dunes, slicing
Up the brindled flat. Here, he will fish

And haul inside spumes of spray – yet for nil.
His blood-boned broken fists cut to white.
He has to get one, just *one*; another empty net and
The birlinn goes next midwinter's night.

The sun sends one promissory note, bringing
A jolt, held breath – then a barely noticed
Sough of air as a fish erupts on deck so strange
That all must laugh or gag or cringe.

A monster – grunion-faced, some rank mix
Of selkie, drowned wean, bloated saithe. The men
Cower back away. It takes the fisherman to crack its skull.
The creature quivers, trembles, dies.

The storm undoes itself. He sails home quite
As cold and lost as any star.
At the door his wife lays her quern-hardened hand
On his back. 'Good my man,' she says.

She guts. They sit knee-to-knee, to sup.
A taste, not unreasonable: oddly, like week-gone
Venison – but spoilt, where the shot went in.
He sleeps a death. The cows in the byre-end

Shuffle and fart. In the fire's done light,
The fisherman's wife examines the glaur worked
In under her nails. There,
A single scale, iridescent, a burning mirror:

Marked with tiny lettering. She takes up her
Looking glass – and sees in hopeful copperplate, there
And on every single scale examined since:
We come in peace.

Corinne Fowler

THE BLACK DEVON

They'd be watching and waiting for her back at the house. Zoë would be twisting her hair by the attic window, listening to the rain and trying to work out what time she must have left. Her mother would have *The Archers* on without listening to it. She'd be sipping black tea without tasting a thing. She could picture her father too, chopping peppers into even slices, marinating the beef. Leaving the room to refill his glass with Old Speckled Hen. And Tomás. He'd be reassuring them that she was just taking a walk, that it was fine to leave her alone. But he wouldn't be watching the news or surfing the internet. And he'd have hidden all the baby clothes at the back of the airing cupboard, lifted the cot into the attic.

Rachael just wandered, long strands of hair clinging to her neck. She didn't scan the wood for startled deer as she usually did. When she reached the stone bridge, she paused to stare into the Black Devon. She just wasn't ready to go back. She moved over to the far side of the bridge and hesitated. Both paths were deep in mud. After a while she set out towards Clackmannan tower. *Clack, clog, stone.* The path lurched up the hill towards the barbed-wire fence. At first she skidded around the edges, her fingernails scraping out tufts of wool from the pockets of her sweater. Soon she needed her hands to stop herself slithering back down the hill. As she climbed, the cedars' red bark rasped against her palms. Then Rachael looked up and saw the tower piercing the ridge ahead.

When the trees stopped, she looked back. They were steaming like a herd of animals in the open fields. The ground oozed mud. Rachael stood flicking the bark and dirt from her fingers. There was a flutter of pigeons. She turned back to face the tower. The rain had picked up. It was pelting onto her scalp, sliding down her cheeks, dripping from her nose and chin. She put her hands back into the woollen pockets, but they were damp. She took them out again and stared at her fingers. They were raw, a flush of pink. She breathed across the numb skin, stretched out her fingers. At least she'd had the presence of mind to wear her walking boots. Zoë would be impressed. She strode uphill towards the tower.

But there was a cold, dead weight curled up inside her. The mud lapped at her boots as she jabbed them into the flabby belly of the hill. The entire slope was liquefying. Marooning her. As she climbed, the view peeped beyond the horizon.

Rachael reached the tower, clung on to the sandstone blocks while the snow-crested hills heaved and fell about her. The tower leaned against her. She craned her neck upwards. Clouds were spilling over the turrets. Her hands dropped to her sides but she knew she had to keep moving. She started walking. Slowly at first, then the grass gathered pace under her boots. Soon she was running along the bony spine of the ridge, laughing and laughing until it juddered inside her chest, tugging at the wires of her throat. Then she was chasing herself round and round the tower, her feet skating over the mud.

Coming to an unsteady halt, she blinked at her mud-spattered clothes and flopped onto her back. The whole tower was spinning out of control, the gargoyles leaning and leering, the giant blocks of stone about to tumble. She rolled onto her belly. The rain drummed onto her head. She tasted grit in her mouth but didn't spit it out, laid her head against the shuddering ground. The landscape was all smeared now, the rain-flattened grass seeping into the curve of the hill, the blades of grass plastered against the horizon the way hair clings to the head of a newborn baby. And while she buried her face in the black soil, the rain slowed and the down-turned mouth of a rainbow appeared above the wood.

She picked herself up and stumbled over to the engraved plaque beneath a snarling pair of gargoyles. 'Clackmannan tower,' she read, 'built in the fourteenth century by the son of Robert the Bruce.' Robert the Bruce. Everyone in history had children. She watched her breath warming the gathering chill. Soon, surely, there would be space for something else. Once she was healthy again. There would be time for thinking about other things.

Tomás tiptoed up the stairs. Zoë was already waiting on the landing. He always said that she had the knack of anticipating him.

'We should call the police,' she said, giving her hair another twist.

'They won't come out till someone's been missing twenty-four hours,' he said, concentrating on keeping a hushed tone. 'We have to look for her ourselves. We'll say we're going to Tesco's.' She nodded, and reached for her coat.

Rachael wouldn't get lost on the way back. She rarely lost her way. But Zoë would have started worrying about her the second they had come back to the empty house. She was bound to look a sight too; pallid, mud-splattered, hunted. She could clean up in the river or, better still, sneak past them into the bathroom

and shout cheerfully through the locked door while she showered.
Rachael turned towards the fading bars of colour arching above
the trees. The woods were darkening like a bruise.

The barbed wire caught her thigh as she swung over the fence.
She didn't stop to examine it. She started slithering down the path.
Then spotted a light flashing through the bars of the trees. There
were two people on the far side of the wood. She wiped her hand
across her face and hair, hoping she'd avoid them, hoping they
wouldn't try to make her stop and talk. She clambered over a damp
log and squelched through some rotting leaves to get a better look.
They were talking, gesticulating, but she couldn't make out any
words. She needed to find the path that curved round the wood
rather than cutting right through it. Just so she didn't have to meet
them. But her legs were shaking and the cut from the barbed wire
was stinging. The hospital had told her to rest. She leant against a
tree for a moment.

A minute later, she stooped under some low branches and
droplets of rain came rolling down the back of her neck. She pulled
the heavy wool sweater around her and groped her way through
mud and branches. She retraced her steps to the river.

The Black Devon trickles right through the wood. Someone
told her once that it got its name from the coal dust that seeped
from the minefields. Black pus weeping from so many scars.
All that digging could take you to Wales and back. Or get you
drowned at the bedrock where they say all the Scottish lochs meet.
Miles and miles down, deeper than Rachael had the power to
imagine. She lingered on the bank, the river holding her gaze. She
wanted to slide down the bank. She wanted to drown in it. Then
there was a quick crash and snap of twigs, some muffled thuds
against fallen branches. She whipped round. Four red deer flashed
through the wood. She stared after them until they faded to specks
of blackness.

There was a snatch of conversation at the edge of the wood.
They were walking along the lower path. Their path would join hers
at any moment. But she couldn't hide in these woods any longer.
Zoë would have got Tomás completely worried by now. Rachael
hoped that it wasn't them, out with a torch in this downpour. She
felt a stab of guilt. Tomás hated the rain. And Zoë didn't deserve
that kind of worry. Ahead the stones of the bridge were glistening
in the dark. Halfway across the bridge she heard the soft hoot of
an owl. She paused to wait for the answering call before she left the
wood. She pulled her wet hair back into a ponytail and headed for
home, back to the hidden cot and the unworn baby clothes.

So this was what it was like to walk in the dark. She'd feared and dreaded it for so long. Nearly everyone dreads it. Once night falls, every tree stump becomes a crouching figure. But now she'd left the wood the estuary came into view. She could see right across the rain-puckered surface to the oil refinery at Grangemouth on the far shore. Its lights were flickering like fireflies in the dark. And, just ahead of her, the torchlight came bumping towards her over the stones.

Ewan Gault

THE RESTLESS WAVE

I'd never been at sea before. Felt sick half the time. This morning I got out of a dead man's bunk and went to the mirror. A face stupid as a stained-glass saint stared back. A spot had sprouted on the side of my nose. I squeezed it between my finger and thumb. The boat rocked, the boat rolled. A rough sea the radio had decreed. The spot burst, yellow pus speckled the dirty mirror.

Uncle Tam clambered into the cabin. I stepped away from the mirror but he had seen me. 'Aye, you've got it,' he said, 'a Campbell's face, no point denying it.' He clamped my cheeks between powerful hands, stepped back and held them up like a man showing the size of the one that got away. I rubbed my jaws. Outside, the boat creaked its way through the empty sea. 'Get that one up,' he said nodding at his son. He climbed back up the wooden steps and I returned to inspecting my face. When my breath had steamed the reflection I let my chapped lips touch the glass.

'The kiss of life.'

'What?'

'You look like death.'

Johnny slithered into a pair of salt-encrusted jeans. 'You should have been on deck twenty minutes ago, your dad was down.'

'Was he fuck.'

He sat picking at the athlete's foot that grew between his toes. Chances were he'd been watching me all this time. He kept the World Service murmuring faint embers of words through the night; the crackle of background gunfire mixing with a dreich evening, news of some distant earthquake and the constant rolling of the boat. He brushed past and as I turned I tried to catch my reflection unawares. From somewhere across the world a bullet cracked a head wide open. The same eyes, the same sallow skin. It wasn't a bad face, but it had fuck all to do with me.

*

Uncle Tam shot the net and we motored along at a couple of knots for three hours. There wasn't anything to do so I got my fishing rod out and cast a line. I stared at the restless waves, worrying a broken tooth, probing its rough edges. It's where I've been all week. Since then it's come out. A new landscape for my tongue.

'Caught anything?' Johnny asked. I stared off at the black hulk of an island, its rocky head rising from the sea. 'The Flannan Isles,' Johnny nodded in their direction. 'Scary place.'

'Imagine living there.'

'Nobody does. Used to, mind, but not any more.' I rubbed my eyes, sure I'd seen three figures high up on the cliffs.

There was a shout from the back of the boat. They were bringing the net in. We walked round to where the rest of the crew stood, waiting and making bets on the size of the catch. My eyes followed lumps of kelp, tangled up in the orange net and dragged from the deep. I stared into the frothy water. Something black and strange was being dredged up.

It hung in front of us. Soft, plump, encased in oilskins and rubber. Only the feet hung out, white, succulent, like one of they shellfish that are only just worth the bother of getting into. I didn't know what to do with my hands. 'A bloody waste ay space,' I'd been called more than once this month. I watched the gows, their chill cries and shocked white wings wheeling away on the wind. I wanted to fold my arms.

A cry grated out of Tam's barnacled throat. Johnny bundled his father into the wheelhouse. He had come back to us. Floating just under the surface, his choked air tubes now open; his body puffed up with gas and saltwater, jellyfish-like, powerless against the currents. I stepped towards the strung-up body. His naked feet hung at the same height as my face, turned in so that one now rested on top of the other. I pulled a strand of seaweed from my cousin Joe's big toe, let it fall amongst the twitching fish beating out their last on the deck. He was dripping on me, his whole oozing body. I took my knife out and cut him from the net.

We wrapped the body in blankets from my bunk and took him to the hold. I kept imagining him at market, sunk in crushed ice. A queer fish, they would say. Men with raw faces would poke and prod, whistle through their teeth. We would hang him up by his feet, weigh him, get our photos taken by his side.

'Stitch.'

'Aye, Uncle Tam.'

'Joe, how was he? How did he seem?'

'Well, he seemed … fine.'

'Peaceful?'

'Aye. Peaceful.'

'Nothing queer about him?'

'Nothing.'

'This is the Lord's work. Joe always was a good loon. His mother will be right glad to have him back.'

He nodded, his eyes drifting in unsettled skies.

The bulging net of the cod-end had been opened and the deck was alive with twitching tails and gasping gills. Cal started sorting the different types of fish while the other deckies stood in a group, gawping into the ends of one another's fags.

'Am I the only one working today?' Cal growled.

I got my knife out and started gutting a box of cod. The others got to it, each going about their business in silence. The fish were freezing, my fingers soon numb. I took off my bloody rubber gloves. The calluses, cuts from the gutting knife, didn't seem part of me. I hid them under my oxsters.

'I cannae take this,' shouted Corky, his ginger head coming out of the hold. 'A'm sorry but one ay yous can do it. Dead bodies, man.' Cal stared at him, embarrassed. Johnny, who was squatting over the side of the boat taking a dump, pulled his oils up and without looking at us headed down to the hold.

I handed Corky my basket of gutted fish, which he washed before throwing the lifeless rubber bodies down the chute to Johnny.

My hands worked on automatic, gutting fish after fish. I stopped for a breather and looked at my pink, shaking hands. I didn't recognize them. The right hand held a knife. It pressed the point of the blade down onto the back of the left hand and scraped it slowly across. A white line appeared along which a few beads of blood threaded themselves. Nobody noticed. I watched them working, in slow motion it seemed, their movements like men underwater. The right hand hacked down. I felt my skin open up, like lips coming unstuck in the morning. The blood, darker than expected, twisted round my wrist. Fell to the deck with the guts of dead fish.

'What have you done?' shouted Cal.

'An accident,' I said 'I'll get it fixed.'

Tam was in the galley with the First Aid box. 'Will you stop bleeding everywhere,' he snapped as I stood pretending to play some ghostly piano, tinkling droplets of blood onto the floor. 'This'll sting a bit.' I felt like telling him that it wouldn't, 'cause that wasn't my hand. It belonged to someone else the moment we left harbour. It fixed nets, scrubbed decks, gutted fish. I couldn't understand how it had got so clever so fast. I watched it crawl around doing strange tasks like a hard, bony insect.

My uncle's eyes dodged this way and that, anything to avoid looking at me. I thanked him and went down the hold to see Johnny.

I thought I heard him talking to himself as I climbed the ladder but there was nothing there but boxes of iced fish. Then through the noise of the engine's dreary drone I heard again, softly spoken words. The tang of brine stung the back of my throat. The fish gaped, unseeing eyes pointing everywhere. I looked at the shape of Joe's body. The voice spoke of water temperatures in the Hebrides, Mallan, of a low moving steadily northeast in Cromarty before losing its identity. I put one hand on the ladder's rung before seeing Johnny's radio, sitting next to the chute.

Joe's cold bony feet peered out from beneath my blankets. The end of his toes had gone a minty green. I put a bunnet on and tried to rub some warmth into myself. His feet were the same as mine, well-shaped with none of the coarse hair that covered the arms and legs of all the men in our family.

Johnny slipped down the ladder and started pacing unsteadily. It was some time before he said, 'You got ma lighter?' I kent his lighter was sitting next to the radio but I just stood there staring at Joe's feet.

'You've hid it, ya wee fucker, haven't you?' I licked my lips. Johnny clenched his eyes, knuckle-white tight. He was older than me, harder than me. He took three jerky steps forwards but stopped at his brother's body.

'You're sweating,' I said. He took a raggedy breath then bent down and tugged the blanket over Joe's feet. 'Mon,' he said, 'Corky needs a hand fixing the net.' We left the body to rest, the radio whispering the horrors of the world into its ears.

*

The next evening we sailed into port, or The Mariner, as Tam bitterly cried it. Cars moved silently along the front as stickmen and women waited on the harbour walls. Johnny leaned over the side, biting hard on his lower lip. 'Can you see any of the family?' I shook my head, blinking at the harsh white ambulance and police car shining in the low light. I wondered if my dad had come down from the Air Force base. He'd been waiting after my first shift but said he'd be too busy this time. I wanted away from the stinking fish and deckies as quickly as possible.

'What are the pigs here for?'

I looked at the drained blue sky, the moon a fingernail clipping of some careless god. I didn't answer. Gows were squawking our arrival to the town and the fisher-folk's houses seemed to have slunk down to the harbour. Crowding around like old wives wi a secret.

My dad wasn't there so after unloading the fish I went back
with Johnny and my uncle to their bit. The moment we got
through the door Tam produced his pipe and flopped in his easy
chair. After a couple of attempts to light it he leant back puffing
a huge claw of smoke into the air. 'There is a god,' he said to the
smoke with grim satisfaction.

He started chewing and puffing away till the silence and
smoke made my eyes water. In the kitchen Aunt Mary shuffled
wordlessly through dinner preparations. I wanted to ask when my
dad would be finished work. I had just finished school and was
staying with him for the summer, but his flat was on the Air Force
base and I couldn't get through security alone. As I cleared my
throat Johnny's foot beat out a warning on the carpet. I sat back,
watching the smoke swell and rise up, as if at any moment it might
break and crash down over us. 'Are you doing anything?' Johnny
asked. I found myself up on my feet, following him out the door.

In front of the closed-down ice-cream shop we met up with
my cousin Dawn and her pal Nicky.

'Jesus, Johnny, I'm sorry,' Nicky said, giving him a squeeze.
She looked up at me, eyes a green so shocking that if you showed
someone a picture of her they'd say it was photoshopped. She
touched the side of my jacket, the purple slash of lipstick on her
face now smiling softly.

We headed out of town past the graveyard with the stones
bearing all of our names.

'There'll have tae be a funeral now. Another ceremony to upset
Mam,' snarled Dawn. I remembered the last one, my Auntie Mary
squawking the hymns, her off-key voice singing bravely above the
rest.

'Eternal father strong to save
Whose arm has bound the restless wave.'

Johnny had stood next to me, his body quivering. He started
making gurgling, giggling sounds. I had placed my hand on his as
he held on to the pew for dear life.

We cut across the golf course and onto the beach. A light
wind was whipping the drizzle into a frenzy. 'C'mon,' said Johnny,
climbing into one of the concrete pillboxes that had been dotted
along the coast during the Second World War. We sat in the box's
frozen, dank air, glad that this one at least didnae smell of pish.
Nicky unzipped her rucksack and I watched her waxy face as she
lit three fat candles. She took out a radio, some tinfoil, a biro tube
and small paper wrap, her heavy-lidded eyes never once looking
up. The radio DJs, an overexcited boy and compliantly amused

girl, discussed the merits of contestants on *Big Brother*. I imagined them cut off from the world in a sealed-tight studio, certain that somewhere out there nameless people were hanging on their every word. I went back to watching Nicky's rodent hands working, her long black fringe swept back from her face. When she was done her lips drooped into a smile.

I felt sorry for her, sorry for all of them. They seemed so much like the second-rate actors that appear in drug awareness videos we got shown at school – their junk shop chic, hair hanging in their eyes. I knew how it was going to end, everyone did. But they didn't seem to have a clue. Johnny was laughing as he showed me the wrap. 'Look. He's used a page fae a scuddie.' I squinted at the picture of some naked girl sucking seductively on her finger. 'It's that attention to detail you have tae appreciate.' He leant back against the wall, nodding.

Nicky stretched out at the back of the pillbox, soft light rippling over her. She was picking up decades of sand that had been blown through the gun slits. She let them drain through her fingers, singing 'Cold, cold sand, never seen the sun.' She smiled sweetly, 'Stitch, come and lie next to me.' I crawled over, resting my cheek on the tufty, dusty fur of her lapel. She always smelt slightly of candles, looked even more impressively bored in their light. Far-gone eyes, breathing smoke through her nostrils, a private smile itching her lips. I dug my fingers into the sand trying to listen to her heart.

Johnny and Dawn sat guard at the gun slits. Outside, the night had become wild. They leant together and I heard Dawn whisper, 'You can do what you want now. He'll give up the trawling. Joe was always the apple of his eye. This'll be too much, even for him.' Johnny hunched back and caught me looking.

'What do you think?'

'There's no money in it, even Tam kens that. He was only keeping on 'cause Joe was into it.' Johnny sucked hard on his long sad face.

'Do you mind the pond in our garden?' he asked. 'When me and Joe were weans, there used tae be goldfish in that pond. Thing was, the pond wasn't that deep and wi all the gows round here the goldfish were always getting eaten. My father though just kept buying more.

'Me and Joe were daft about them. Each time he came home wi a new bag we would spend ages fighting over their names. Every so often my father would ask which ones had died. None of the fish lasted long apart from this one called Nessie. He had come in

the first bag of fish and Joe had named him. He was our favourite.
Every morning we would rush out. "Is he gone?" "I can't see him,
wait, there he is behind the rock." "Where, are you sure, is that
really him?" "Aye."
'My father started asking after Nessie, laughing and saying
"He's a lucky one that." Well, one day he asked Joe how Nessie
was and Joe just shrugged and said that for all he knew Nessie had
died months ago. See we couldn't make out the difference. From
outside the pond they all looked the same. My father just nodded
and said Joe was probably right. I knew he was right and all but it
didn't stop me hating both of them for it. After that we stopped
checking on the fish and my father stopped buying them.'
    We sat deep in candle-flicker silence. Johnny stretched out his
feet so that they rested on mine. I watched his face, bleached and
knotted as if it had been carved from one of they logs that travel
the sea for years before being thrown up by a storm. 'You got any
left, Nicky?' He heated the tinfoil, sucking greedily on the coil of
smoke as it twisted and squirmed into the plastic tube. A Tornado
from RAF Lossie tore across the sky. We peered out. A second one
followed, with its grotesque plumage of bombs and missiles.
    'It's the end of the world,' Johnny murmured from deep within
the box.
    'Where do you think they're going?' Dawn asked.
    No one answered. It was too mad to think of some loon the
same age as us surrounded by glowing buttons and dials and
millions of pounds' worth of technology. 'Does your dad fly them?'
Nicky asked.
    'No, he's too old,' I replied, 'he's an instructor now.'
    We hung out of the pillbox, watching the plane's lights until
they disappeared in murky skies.
    'Mon,' said Nicky, 'the rain's almost off. Let's get out of here.'
    'Aye c'mon, John, we could look for shells to put on Joe's
grave,' said Dawn. Johnny hawked and spat. 'Stitch, tell him. It's
too cold to sit here all night.' I just shrugged, playing wi the sand,
piling little mounds of it on the end of my trainers. When I looked
up the girls had gone. I stuck my head out the box and watched
them heading towards town, Nicky stepping along the concrete
blocks that had been sunk in the sand to stop the invading army
that never came.
    'We're the last buggers on earth,' Johnny whispered, 'listen
now.' He turned the radio's tuning dial from side to side. One
wave of static after another rolled over us. He smiled, fat yellow
teeth, burnt-bin-bag breath. 'Do you think they know?' His eyes

close to me peered into mine. The same sallow face, same shadow eyes. He turned the volume on the radio right up high so the static sounded like rain on tin roofs, the noise of pins and needles. I held his hand and watched the stumpy candles shiver and gasp. He kissed me on the cheek and we curled up together listening to the hush of the radio, the rush of the sea, telling each other to be quiet.

Diana Hendry

SOME OF THESE DAYS

Mother loves a lady called Sophie Tucker. Sophie Tucker is a big fat lady who sings. Mother says she also 'shimmies' which I think means she shakes her fat about her as if she were playing hoola hoop – only without the hoop.

Mother sits at the piano and plays and sings Sophie Tucker's songs. There is one she particularly likes. It's called *Some of These Days*. Mother sings it to Father. She turns her face towards him, even though his face is covered in newspaper and he's pretending not to listen.

Some of these days, Mother sings, *You're going to miss me, honey!*

She rocks on the piano stool. Her left hand vamps away without her even thinking about it. Without her even knowing. I watch the glint of her gold wedding ring that she rubs on my eye when I have a stye.

Mother is all dark curls and crimson lips. She's wearing a dress that makes me think of a hot country full of vivid flowers. Somewhere like Italy. She tells Father that she's a *red hot momma* and he's *gonna miss her some of these days*. Secretly I know that she's *my* red hot momma not his. And I'm worried.

Someone is leaving and I'm not sure who it is.

You'll be so lonely, for me only, Mother sings. And it brings the tears to my eyes because I know I would be. I think I'd just slowly shrivel up like an apple left to rot in the bowl, starting with my skin. Then I'd shrink and shrink until I vanished. Not even the core of me left. Mother has that.

Apart from the black wing of the baby grand piano that's in the bay window, our sitting room is all beige and cream. The walls, the carpet, the sofa, the chairs. It's a room doing its best to be very quiet and well-behaved. *How nice!* visitors say when they come in. Then they lower their voices. Still, Mother blooms in here, like an exotic pot plant. Mother never lowers her voice. Or her laugh. She has a laugh that makes Lal, my sister, wince.

Not that we have many visitors. Those we do have are usually business acquaintances of Father's who need to be entertained. Sometimes I think that the whole house is the way it is – the velvet curtains, the chandelier, the cream and the beige – for the entertainment of the acquaintances.

Mother says that when she was a girl, people just called in. They didn't wait to be invited. And the samovar was always on.

Perhaps it's Father who's leaving. Going off with the acquaintances.

And when you leave me, be sure it's gonna grieve me, Mother sings to him. She doesn't sound sad about it. She doesn't sound *grieving.* She sounds really happy about it, that left hand of hers bouncing up and down on the keyboard, her right foot on the loud pedal that's as gold as her wedding ring.

Father rustles his newspaper. He doesn't look as if he's leaving. He sits in that armchair every night except Thursdays when he's very late home and Mother lets me stay up late while she wanders about the house. After I've gone to bed she sits in the dark in the front bedroom, watching for him. Perhaps that's when he's leaving. On Thursday. I wouldn't mind too much.

There's other Sophie Tucker songs that Mother sings.

A good man, is hard to find
You always get the other kind.
Just when you think that he's your pal
You turn around and find him flirting with another gal.

This could be another hint about Father leaving. But I don't think so because Mother is always telling Lal, Mags and me that Father is a good man and that we've each to find one.

A good man, according to Mother, is one who is honest and ambitious. He's a man who wants to 'get on'. Every morning Mother sends Father forth looking very important (because that's how you have to look to get on) in his laundered shirt and expensive suit and polished shoes, his moustache trimmed, his tummy full of bacon and eggs and black pudding.

It's a great relief when we hear him drive out of the garage and away, getting on for us. Something in me thinks that Mother may have got things wrong about a good man, only I'm not certain what it is.

And now, with the sun dancing into the breakfast room, where the acquaintances never come, Mother and I are alone at last. Mother can drink her tea and then, while washing the dishes, sing *After You've Gone* or *You made me love you, I didn't wanta do it, I didn't wanta do it* as loudly as she likes, and I can play with my fatherless paper dolls in the tasselled tablecloth tent under the table.

Mags has been sent away to boarding school because Father thinks she's stupid and because she gets on his nerves. Mags has frizzy hair and buck teeth and a lot of spots, so even though she sings like an angel it's unlikely she'll find a good man or a bad one. Lal has gone off to work at the salon. Lal is tall and slim and superior. She rides a double-decker bus into town like Boadicea.

Lal despises Sophie Tucker. She shows me photographs of her in a magazine she has. 'She's gross,' Lal says. 'Vulgar.' Lal says the word 'vulgar' as if she's got something nasty in her throat. Lal herself is concentrating on being either smart, in her black suit for the double-decker bus, or romantic in lilac gingham. Sophie Tucker is wearing a pink feather boa, something matchingly fluffy on her head, a dress that's all spangles and has a slit almost up to her waist and a big smile. I think she looks wonderful. I understand instantly what people mean when they say of someone *larger than life*. I look at Sophie Tucker and feel as if I'm expanding inside in a way I can't explain and which has nothing to do with being fat.

'She tells terrible jokes,' Lal says gloomily because she seems to recognise that she's living in a shameful family with Mother, me and Sophie Tucker and that she'd like to ride away on the double-decker and never come back. She won't tell me any of the jokes.

'Sophie Tucker,' I say. 'It's a nice name.' This is a bit lame, I know, but I want to defend Sophie while acknowledging Lal's superior nature and without risking one of Lal's tortures, like Chinese wrist burn or nettle whipping which is something Lal does to my legs when I disturb her in the garden. Anyway, it's true. I do think Sophie Tucker is a lovely name. I wish it was mine. Sometimes I say the name over and over to myself in bed at night, just for the prettiness of 'Sophie' and the snug tucked-inness of 'Tucker'.

Lal sighs. 'Brazen,' she says. 'And brassy.' I add both words to my treasure store because they both shine like gold. Lal buttons her blouse up to her throat and goes off to her room where I am not allowed. At other times she separates herself from Mother and me by locking herself in the greenhouse with a bag of apples and an historical novel from the library that's wrapped in cellophane so you can't really feel the book.

After Father and Lal have gone to work, Mother and I have the day to ourselves. Firstly we shop. This is an outing for which we both dress up even though we're only going to the local village shops. In the summer Mother wears one of her flamboyant dresses and her white sandals and sometimes a floaty scarf round her neck. I wear one of the dresses she's made for me which has a frill on the bodice, my white socks and my sandals that have a pattern of daisies stamped out on the toes. Mother carries her basket. It's a married woman's basket and Mother is very proud of it. Nobody else, none of the other mothers out shopping, look as bright and proud as Mother and for that matter none of them laugh as loudly. I can always find her by her laugh. Sometimes Mother tries to talk to the other mothers but she never seems to have much luck. 'Good morning,' is about all she gets back.

'Snooty,' Mother says and saves her laughter for Mrs Billings in the grocer's or Mr Thomas in the newsagent's.

We spend the summer afternoons on the beach. Mother packs the picnic basket (it has blue plastic handles) with a thermos of orange juice and packet of jam sandwiches. Then we're off. We have to go past the row of little houses called prefabs which I think are very pretty but Mother says, 'Cheap and tinny – be glad you don't live in one.' Then we hurry past the waste ground where a bomb once fell on our village. Mother won't look at it because you never know when a bomb might fall and she won't let me look in the air-raid shelter on the sand-dunes in case I get trapped inside.

The beach is only five minutes away but when we're there it's as if we've travelled to another country, a secret country which we never tell Father or Lal about. There's something secretly a bit wicked about our visits to the beach. Maybe it's because we know Father is out there, getting on, and Lal is in her hot salon trying to make people beautiful who don't start off that way and poor Mags is locked up in a boarding school far, far away.

Mother spreads out a rug and takes off her stockings. I'm free to paddle or make a castle or dig for Australia which is what I like doing most, feeling sure that I'll dig deep enough one day and will see people walking upside down.

We're always home in time for Mother to cook the dinner and I'm always surprised that Father and Lal can't tell from our faces that we've been away in a foreign country where happiness lives.

In the winter it's different. Mother lights the fire in the afternoon and sits in the big armchair. She takes off her roll-on which is a tight rubbery band she wears to keep her tummy in. Sometimes we play shops. I fetch all her shoes and pretend to be the shop assistant. More often she tells me stories about when she was a child and about her five brothers and sisters and mad Aunt Fanny who sat under the piano and wouldn't come out and Louis and Reuben who were always going off to the races and gambling, and her father who was a tailor and had a lot of cronies he liked to play cards with at night, clearing the tailoring tables and sending Mother out for whisky.

And I wish I could live in that house with the brothers and mad Fanny and be sent out in the night to buy whisky because it all sounds much more exciting than living here behind our net curtains and with a father who is good.

Come six or seven in the evening, I have to give her up to him. She's away to the bedroom to pretty herself up, dab her cheeks with rouge and put on fresh lipstick. Then she puts his slippers out on the hearth to warm and has his dinner ready and waiting. After that she's all his. She ruffles his hair and says *Tell me you love me, Harry. Tell me.* And he does even if his voice sounds somehow flat. But Mother seems satisfied so perhaps this is the best you can expect from a good man after a day getting on.

I'm not sure where Lal is. Either she's shut up in her bedroom or out with one of her many beaus, though we know she hasn't found the right one yet.

Then Father settles in his armchair with his newspaper and I curl up on the sofa and it's time for the piano and Sophie Tucker.

Kate Hendry

THE COOP

The first time they chose a lodger Annie went for the one she liked best, not the one who would stay the longest. Liking was no use. Mum's advert in the *Gazette* had been all wrong too. 'Room to rent,' it had said, 'in large, beautiful house, with small friendly family, cat and dog. Close to town centre.' It should have said what sort of lodger they wanted and that they couldn't up and leave when they felt like it. They'd argued for ages over each word. Mum had fought for 'beautiful'. 'I want someone with a sense of aesthetics,' she'd said. Gordon had said they'd end up with someone hairy and into flowers. And he only wanted to be friendly when he felt like it. Annie had wanted to put 'women only'.

'I don't want to live with a man,' she'd said.

'What about me?' said Gordon.

'You don't count. You're not a proper grown-up.'

Gordon had snorted.

'You lived with your father,' said Mum. 'For years. It wasn't that long ago he left.'

'Well I don't want another man.' That was as firm as she could be, but they'd still ignored her.

Mum had said she could choose a question for the interview though. She and Gordon could have one each. Gordon had wanted to have 'do you shag a lot?' but Mum said he couldn't ask that.

'We could ask "will your partner be staying over?"' she suggested.

'Are you going to let them?' Annie wanted to know. She wasn't sure about having two people in the room opposite hers. She might bump into one of them, the extra one, on the stairs. What if they had no clothes on?

'It's the eighties,' Mum said. 'We won't get a lodger at all if we say no partner.'

There was no way round it. One way or another there would be a man in the house. Which was worse? A boyfriend sneaking round the house half-naked in the dark when you didn't even know he'd come back for the night, or a full-time man lodger? She'd just have to not get up in the night. A good question could put off a potential man lodger. 'Who would you rather be, Cagney or Lacey?' She was pleased with that – they wouldn't want to be either, even though being a detective was a man's job really, they were still both women.

In the end only one man phoned up and Mum didn't like the sound of him so she told him the room was gone. Annie was glad. It must have been the word 'beautiful' that did it. Maybe it had put off lots of women too – there had only been two candidates. The first was Margy. 'Fat Margy', Gordon called her. 'She's just short,' Mum said, 'it makes her look round.' She'd liked her because she liked Radio Four and she wore frilly knickers. 'I don't want to *know* that,' said Gordon, 'it's disgusting, she's too fat.' Annie thought he was being mean, she couldn't help being fat. Though really she was too old for frilly knickers, she must have been at least thirty-five, maybe even forty. And she said she wanted to be Cagney, which was completely the wrong answer, especially at her age. Mum still wanted to be Cagney too. Annie kept telling her she couldn't be but she wouldn't listen. Mum liked Margy but she agreed not to have her, if they didn't like her.

So then there was only Belinda and they had to all like her as there wasn't anyone else. Gordon asked her if she had a boyfriend. She did and they were supposed to be living together but the house wasn't ready. Robin (the boyfriend) had said he'd do it up but he was always too busy. So they'd been living with his parents and she was fed up with it. Fed up with him, thought Annie, he sounded like a total waste of space, Belinda would be better off with them. They'd make her feel better. But then it didn't sound like she needed cheering up, she had such a busy life. She went out with friends from work on Friday night (Gordon wanted to know what pub. It was the Swan – his favourite), Robin on Wednesday and Saturday. On Sunday she spent the day with him and the evening at his parents one week and hers the next. She wasn't usually in before ten o'clock. One night a week she went out with one of her old school friends. Robin got a lot of her time, considering she was fed up with him. She did say she'd rather be Lacey but what was the point when she'd probably not be in on the night it was on anyway?

Mum had to consult the *I Ching*. Should they go for Belinda or re-advertise? Should they have a lodger at all? Mum always got like this – she'd be just on the edge of making a decision and she'd get panicky and not want to think about it at all. Gordon said it was a cop out – why couldn't she make her own decision for once? Mum said the *I Ching* was a book of wisdom – he shouldn't be so disrespectful. Annie liked the coins, the Chinese letters on each side, the square hole in the middle. They all liked to watch them fall, to work out the hexagrams. Gordon wouldn't stop scoffing, but he always stuck around for the verdict.

You had to get the question right. If the answer didn't make sense then maybe you hadn't asked the right question. Mum had to work out the question in her head. She wouldn't say what it was until after she'd thrown the coins. She'd be asking it over and over again as she rattled them. Sometimes she let Annie write down the lines. Once they'd got them all she'd reveal the question. This time it was 'How Do I Allow Lodgers into My Home?' 'Aren't you going to ask if Belinda's the right one?' asked Annie. 'Too obvious,' said Mum, 'anyway, it's not about her, it's about me.' 'I thought you were going to ask if we should have them at all,' said Gordon, sounding relieved. He wanted lodgers, as long as they'd get him into the pub.

Mum worked out the hexagram and read it out. It was 'Holding Together'. Did that mean yes to lodgers or that they had to stick together as a family, with no intruders? It was hard to tell. It always was with the *I Ching*. Mum read some more:

'"What is required is that we unite with others. Such holding together calls for a central figure. To become a centre of influence is a grave matter and requires greatness of spirit."'

'That'll be you then,' said Gordon to Mum.

'It's a serious business,' agreed Mum, 'taking on such a role. "The centre of influence." I suppose we might have young people. You know, ones who are easily led.'

'Led into what?' Annie wanted to know but they wouldn't say.

'You'll be like their role model,' said Gordon, 'just think of all the books you could get them to read.' Gordon really wanted lodgers, he hated Mum's kind of books normally; all those stories.

'You can keep her in line,' said Gordon. 'That's what a good landlady does.'

Mum laughed but they could tell she was pleased. The *I Ching* had come up with a good answer. It was the 'greatness of spirit' that did it. And Gordon – he was good at getting people to do what he wanted.

Belinda arrived with two suitcases of clothes, one suitcase with bathroom stuff and makeup and a box full of pandas. She hadn't said anything about the pandas when she'd come for her interview and she must have seen Annie's panda, he was always downstairs somewhere. Gordon had a panda too, but his sat on a shelf in his room. Annie said about Panda as soon as she saw Belinda's box.

'D'you want to see my collection?' asked Belinda, beginning to unpack it onto the kitchen table. There were fourteen bears.

'These are the highlights,' said Belinda, 'the rest are in my mum and dad's loft. I've got forty-three in total.'

Annie had a good look at them. She wasn't sure if they were the kind of bears you could pick up or if Belinda would let her. None was as nice as Panda. She showed him to Belinda.

'He's got clothes on,' said Belinda. 'You shouldn't let them wear clothes, it's not natural. And his colours are the wrong way round, he's not a real panda. See,' she said pointing to the largest in her collection, 'black round the eyes, black ears, black legs with the colour sweeping up round the shoulders.'

Belinda also had three panda mugs, four pairs of panda socks, all unworn, ten panda badges, a panda clock and panda slippers. 'I wear them on special occasions,' she told them. She lined up her collection on the bookshelves in her room, moving the small selection of books to a corner of the room. Mum and Annie had picked them together. Annie's favourite was *Little Women*.

Belinda made her room look nice and tidy very quickly. She had her own bedspread and cushions to go on top, so her bed became a sofa during the day. She had a stereo and a portable TV too. Annie hoped this wouldn't mean she'd spend all her evenings in her room. The few that were left after she'd been out most nights of the week.

It worked out all right in the end – Belinda had tea with them nearly every week – usually on a night she was working late and she got home tired and couldn't be bothered to cook. She started to bring a bottle of wine for Mum, and a Fudge bar for Annie. After tea Belinda would hold up a dishcloth and a tea towel. 'Wash or dry,' she'd say, 'you choose.' Annie always chose drying-up, but Belinda always asked – it was just how they did it. Drying-up was the best because you could race the washing-up person but the washing-up person had to rinse as well so the drying-up person always won. Gordon put things away. That was the quickest job but not so good because you couldn't join in the conversation so easily. Mum sat at the table with a cigarette and another glass of wine. Over the washing-up Belinda would complain about Robin and the house – how he still hadn't done the wiring or how he still hadn't started the plastering. Every week there was a list of jobs he hadn't finished. Should they sell up, she wondered? Things were getting bad, Annie could tell Robin would not last much longer.

Annie and Mum sometimes walked past the house with the dog, on the way to the park. Castro was Gordon's dog and he did most of the walking but sometimes Mum and Annie would do it and that's the way they'd go. It was a white cottage, on its own, opposite the cemetery. Annie always looked out for Robin but he was never there. The path squeezed between the house and an old arched corrugated-iron shed, all rusty red and falling apart. It went with the house, it belonged to it.

Mum said the shed looked like an air-raid shelter, like the one from when she was a child, when her whole street would pack in. This one had had its door ripped off by the bomb. If you'd been the last one in, that would have been the end of you. Dad used to say it wasn't an air-raid shelter at all but a chicken coop, hundreds of them packed inside, roosting, never allowed out. The fox would pace round and round, night after night, until one night he was so hungry he leapt at the coop and broke the door down. The hens didn't know about the outside, they didn't know how to escape so the fox caught them all. He killed them and ate every one. There was just a pile of red bloody feathers left, Dad said. Annie always thought about looking inside – maybe there would be something left – a bit of bomb or someone's shoe that had been flung off in the blast. Or maybe feathers, probably half rotted by now. There might be something that would decide it one way or the other – coop or air-raid shelter. But the fence along the path had barbed wire curled round the top and anyway, you'd have to go right inside to see anything – it would be no use peering from the doorway, it would be too dark inside.

'The house is about as bad inside as that shed,' Belinda told them one evening over the washing-up. 'The only thing it's got that the shed hasn't is four walls.' Belinda didn't know the shed was a coop. Or an air-raid shelter. She didn't know the stories. Annie had thought about telling her – she should know about all that had happened there, if she was going to live right next door. But then the stories wouldn't come right in her head and she didn't want Belinda to think she was making them up. Anyway, she wasn't *really* going to move into the little white house, not with Robin in charge of the work.

'What should I do?' Belinda was asking Mum, 'should I tell him I want to sell up?'

'Do you still love him?' asked Mum. He sounded so annoying to Annie, surely Belinda was *completely* fed up with him by now. But 'Yes,' she wailed, scrubbing even harder at the pan.

'Love is not enough,' said Mum, taking another sip of wine. Annie nodded seriously. 'Let's ask the *I Ching*,' said Mum.

'I've heard of that,' said Belinda, 'it's Chinese, isn't it?'

'It's a book of wisdom,' said Mum.

'No pandas,' said Gordon.

'No, I'd know about the pandas, if it had some. Still, Chinese is good.'

Annie went to get the book and the coins. She rattled them gently in her hand as she took them back, whispering her own instructions; 'tell her to sell, tell her to leave him, tell her to sell.' They were warm when she handed them to Belinda. She threw the coins and Mum wrote down the hexagram. Belinda had got 'Work on What Has Been Spoiled'. She grimaced.

'It's not that bad,' said Mum. '"What has been spoiled through man's fault can be made good again through man's work,"' she read. 'That means there's hope.'

'But it's up to Robin,' said Annie, 'he's the man, it says it's his fault and he has to fix it.'

'That's the whole point,' said Belinda, 'he won't do anything.'

'Man can mean woman too, it's just the way the *I Ching* talks. You could be the one that needs to do the work.'

Gordon thought it meant Belinda had to get her hands dirty. 'How come Robin has to do all the hard work?' he asked. Gordon liked Robin. He was always saying Robin should just chuck her. 'I bet she's a rubbish shag,' he'd said once, 'too straight.' He'd helped Robin lay floorboards one weekend. Robin had taken him to the pub afterwards.

'What else does it say?' asked Annie, getting them back to the point.

'"We must not recoil from work but must take hold energetically."'

'I've been trying to tell him this for months but it just goes in one ear and out the other.'

'We should read it to him,' Annie nodded.

'I think it might mean work on the relationship, not the house,' suggested Mum.

It was so annoying. Nobody seemed to realise that Robin was a waste of space. Gordon wouldn't listen.

'All this talking – it's so bourgeois.' That was Gordon's new thing. Everything was bourgeois. He got it from Dad. They'd both joined the Communist Party. Mum said Dad wasn't a communist, he was just stingy. Annie and Mum were trying to ignore the whole thing.

'You've got a six in the fourth place,' said Mum, 'let's see what that means. "Someone is too weak to take measures against decay. If this continues, humiliation will result."'

'That doesn't sound good at all,' said Annie. 'Humiliation.' She said the word as slowly as she could.

'Capitalist decadence,' said Gordon, 'it can only lead to decay.'

Mum frowned at them both, as if she was being as stupid as Gordon.

'What it means is that *he's* the weak one and that *you* have to be strong.'

'What was your question?' asked Annie. Maybe that would stop Mum making up happy endings. She never normally liked them. Especially the love ones.

'It was "should I stay with him?" And I'm no nearer knowing, am I?' She buried her hands in her lap and looked even more upset. Mum put her arm round her.

'Ask another question,' said Annie. Maybe the coins would come up with something really bad this time, like 'Splitting Apart' or 'Oppression', they were the worst ones, Mum always dreaded them. But Belinda wanted to have a lie down in her room. Later she was on the phone to Robin for nearly a whole hour. Surely the 'For Sale' sign would go up soon.

After that Belinda spent more evenings at home. She said she had to save money. Divorce was expensive, Annie knew that. Probably splitting up was too. Sometimes on Saturdays, when Belinda was free, they went out together. That was if Robin hadn't come to get her first. Somehow he was round more often than before. Mum and Dad had done that too, talked more when they'd decided to split up.

On the Saturdays she got Belinda to herself, they went window-shopping. They looked at the cakes they wanted to eat in the bakery and the clothes they liked in the precinct. The kitchen shop, at the top of the high street, was their favourite and they couldn't resist going in. They never once managed to go into that shop without Belinda coming out with something. 'Just a little thing,' she'd say, refusing to let Annie see. She was embarrassed, that was it, buying for a house she had to sell. Annie felt sorry for her. Once it was something Annie spotted and she didn't blame Belinda for buying it – a panda pepper grinder. You turned its head to make it work.

Mum and Annie took Castro out for a walk on Sunday – Gordon was away visiting Dad and he didn't want Annie coming too. They'd be going on a march anyway which was boring. They went on the usual walk. Belinda's house looked even whiter than before – bright white.

'Robin's been here,' said Annie, 'he's painted it.'

'He's been working hard since Belinda had that chat with him,' said Mum.

A coat of paint ready for the sale, that would be it.

'All the inside though, he won't have got round to it.'

'They've been doing it together.' Mum was talking softly and looking at her. She only did it when there was bad news, to stop Annie getting upset.

'D'you want to peer in?' Mum asked. 'Belinda said we could have a peek if we were passing.' She was talking even more quietly than before, like it might keep Annie quiet too.

'They're moving in a fortnight,' she said.

There were curtains in the windows, neatly looped to the sides. When had Belinda chosen them? They had a horrible red and black wavy pattern.

'It's just the right size for the two of them,' Mum was saying.

Belinda had told Mum first and then she'd got Mum to tell Annie.

And she'd been buying stuff in secret. She'd never get to see the panda pepper grinder working now. Mum would be back on the washing-up and the chat wouldn't be the same and there'd be empty Saturdays again.

'I wanted her to stay too,' said Mum following her down the path. 'I'm sure you can come to visit.'

She walked away from Mum and the curtains and stopped at the fence. The barbed wire was gone. There was nothing to stop her climbing over to look at the coop. It had been fixed up and painted. The end wrecked by the bomb, or flattened by the fox, had been bricked up and a new door fitted – a normal shed door, small and narrow with a padlock. Belinda and Robin had put two windows into the wall and for the first time Annie could see inside the coop – she could see how they had made it empty.

Nick Holdstock

WHAT PRACTICE MAKES

Miss Adams asked what she'd been practising. Ruth began to play, arms extended, back straight, while Miss Adams sat. They stayed that way for seven minutes, neither noticing the kitchen sounds (plate on plate, some solid *chops*) or from further, in the yard, the back and forth of Daddy's saw on the dead elm tree.

Ruth sounded the last D sharp, let the key rise with her finger. The note lodged in the walls and floor, in the cameo at Miss Adams' throat. It curled and got comfy.

Ruth counted three, four, had got to six when Miss Adams said, 'You began that well.' She blushed, because Miss Adams meant this as a compliment. Beginnings were very important to her: if things were going to finish well, they had to start out right.

Of course Miss Adams said other things. That Chopin had not meant the middle part to be a race; that she had got two bars confused (and here Miss Adams stood and walked to the piano, and this was a rare privilege, because she did not usually like to play). She ended, as she often did, by saying, 'It is not just the notes. There is also the *feeling*.'

But Ruth knew she *had* done well, because then Miss Adams asked what she would like to learn next. And although this wasn't a real question, Ruth answered truthfully. Miss Adams looked out the window, where the sky and few remaining leaves calmly returned her gaze. It would be a good sunset, one, perhaps, to watch.

Miss Adams said, 'No. That's too difficult.' Because of course there was an order, a sequence to learning, and you could not jump this queue any more than you could start to climb a mountain from halfway.

Ruth nodded, said, 'Yes, Miss Adams.' She did not protest that she had already bought the music. If Miss Adams said it was too hard, she was certainly right.

*

At school Ruth was told about the First World War. Mr Matthews paced and spoke of trenches, gas, who was on whose side. He said, 'Never before had people died in their millions.' He sounded angry about it.

After lunch Carmen told her she had a crush on Luke. 'Why?' said Ruth and Carmen replied she liked the shape of his nose.

Ruth's hair was still damp from the pool when she set off for home. Wind hurried the smaller clouds and bent the branches back. The sky was purple slashed as she entered the park. She smelt the smoke of leaf bonfires and turned right at the swings. And she had heard the Ashkenazy recording, its haste and its precision. It was difficult, but surely, it couldn't hurt to try.

So after dinner, after grammar, Ruth opened the score. She smoothed her eyes from left to right, felt her fingers tense. She read on, past the opening, through the first climb, to the movement's end. Her teeth pressured her lips. She thought she maybe could. The problem would be the changes, they looked way too fast.

But when Ruth went downstairs, into the small, high-ceilinged room, this was not the piece she started. Instead she began the Liszt Miss Adams had prescribed. She made mistakes – sharps not flats, missed and added notes – but carried on regardless. That way she had the whole of it, not perfect little parts. She played it twice more, each time working on the problems, tugging at the knots. She liked it, it was nice. But it didn't matter.

*

She woke to the sound of rain, a gentle pattering. She had been on the beach; swimming in the ocean. That was all she could remember, and when her mother knocked, three soft raps, Ruth said she was awake. She got up, washed her face, combed her brown hair smooth.

When she entered the kitchen her father said, 'Good morning.' Her mother was boiling eggs. Ruth buttered her toast and then her mother gave them their eggs. When Ruth removed the top of hers, it smelt of baby birds, the fume cupboards from Chemistry. She said she wasn't hungry, that she would be late. After a lecture, then a glass of milk, she was allowed to leave.

It wasn't real rain. Apart from the roads – black and shiny – there wasn't much, not enough for umbrellas. As she walked to school, past the old church, past the sweet shop, all the car tyres said *shush*. She thought of the opening bars. And when Mr Webb asked someone to draw the stamen and pistil, while she kept watch as Carmen tried to steal make-up, Ruth saw the notes, her hands.

But her hands had to be washed. They had to lay the table. They had to be folded for Grace; to hold the knife that cut the meatloaf that was just okay. They had to draw the Niger delta; graph the mean expenditure of farmers B and C. Finally, just after nine, Ruth descended the stairs softly, almost on tiptoe. She heard a news voice say, *nuclear*, her father's quick answer. She closed the thick door, raised the wooden lip. She sat, opened the score, then sat some more, her pulse quicker, her ears working hard. So long as she was practising, her mother (who only knew a little Schubert) wouldn't say anything. Ruth straightened and began.

*

The sun sliced through, a late fly buzzed, baffled but resigned. She woke. She yawned and stretched in a happy, not-a-school-day manner. She thought, If I had a cat, would it be here now? What would it be called?

A smell of smoke, the woody kind, brought her to the window. Her father, his lips pursed, was sweeping, burning leaves. Ruth yawned again. She had played long after her bedtime, and if it had been reading or TV, they would have said something.

The fly started to sound pathetic. She lifted the window, tried to shoo it out. It recoiled from the cold air, made for the warm centre. And the beginning was definitely a problem: a downhill with no brakes; so steep it was falling.

Ruth heard her name called. 'Honey, we're going shopping.' She heard her reply, the pause, then the door shutting. The engine started, and she stood, hearing the sound recede. Ruth put on her dressing gown; pushed her feet into slippers; softly padded downstairs.

A tap was dripping in the kitchen where the chrome was gleaming. She poured herself some milk, drank half of it, then refilled the glass. The piano room was as she'd left it, the lid up, the score on the stand. She turned to the first page. And even though she knew this part, her eyes joined the dots. Perhaps she had missed something. But no, these were all the notes; the way that it should sound.

So she tried again, cautiously, her hands trying to think ahead, her legs a little cold. At first things were fine, her fingers ran but managed to keep pace. She was halfway down when she stumbled, and when that happened, she looked back, then down, which made her falter more; by the bottom of the page her confidence was bruised.

But she had been trained to play on, to not quit when behind. She slipped, she lurched, but eventually, the piece began to level off and then, as if emerging from a ravine, things started to open. The notes began to flow and merge; their torrent slowed to a stream. Ruth walked along its looping banks, through a lush, well-watered valley, the sun spring-bright, the slow stream purling on. Her fingers followed the course, its grand meander, gentle sweeps, the lazy snake of it. Then the key bit through the lock, and there were feet and voices. She started, loudly said, 'I'm here.' The feet approached. 'Heavens, you're not even dressed.' She half turned. 'Sorry, I've been practising.' Her mother said, 'Well, that's good,' while her father, unseen, looked to God.

On Sunday they went for a drive. They had a picnic; sat in what was left of fall; wood-walked on the leaf carpet; met other families and dogs. Ruth walked behind her parents, looking at the scattered silver, fallen gold: the devalued currency of 1969.

Then it was back to school. On Monday she had orchestra. They were warned about a charity concert. They practised 'The Thieving Magpie'.

When she got home she was tired and had a lot of French.

She did not attempt it next day either. She did not lack the time (Math had been cancelled), or the inclination. It was because she had her lesson tomorrow. If she practised it now her efforts might leave a trace, an echo that the highly trained ear of Miss Adams might catch. And if she knew that Ruth had disobeyed her, attempted peaks as well as hills, she would say (as she had on the only occasion when Ruth was unprepared) how *very* disappointed she was. So Ruth did not try the descent again. Instead she tinkled out the Liszt, its little chirping sounds. She worked hard on it, made progress, so much that Miss Adams spoke of her playing it in the winter County Contest. But despite all this, despite having done nothing wrong, Ruth was happy when the clock chimed eight.

*

The first snow fell at dawn, piling fast enough to evoke cries of wonder, shakes of head, in the just-woken young and old. Milk was heated, hats put on, and then, the flakes abruptly stopped without a by-your-leave. The sky began to clear, to blue; the sun said *false alarm*.

Ruth walked along the kerb, wondering what shape her body would make; would there be a general flattening or just a Ruth-shaped hole? Meanwhile the spades bit and scraped, clearing paths, suggesting, if she wanted to, she had better hurry.

And why couldn't she play it? It wasn't impossible. Many people could. Six weeks, and still she fell each time. Sometimes she got in sight of the river's coils. But that was when she'd lose her footing, when her hands would trip.

She stepped over a patch of ice; heard distant shouts of throwing. She would only play the beginning. Only when she had that right, only after a proper descent; only then would she allow herself to walk beside the stream.

The bell was ringing when she got to school. Ruth knocked the snow from her shoes then went inside, down the corridor, into her homeroom. Carmen was there already, and Sue-Anne, and Lucille, and Miss Fender in two sweaters, looking up, making a green tick next to *Ruth*.

The room filled. A second bell rang. Miss Fender said, 'All of you should pay attention. Today's assembly will be special.' Then she stood up, walked towards the door, and they all did the same. They filed out, turned left, walked down the corridor. They curved round to the right, a little troop not quite in step, Miss Fender leading, thinking *Bob should buy another*.

They entered the hall and walked past orange rows. When they reached the black chairs they sat and this was the signal for Mrs Gramm to start. And for the first few notes Ruth was convinced that she was playing *her* piece, and nothing would have been more unfair. To have to hear her mangle pieces she knew she could play better: this was bad enough. But for her to somehow be able to play a piece so obviously beyond her, for this to be the rule's exception: this would be too much.

But no, old Gramm was just rushing the allegro of the Grieg in G. Ruth folded her hands and watched the other classes enter. The orange filled, and then the black. The hall was bright with chatter. Then the principal came forward and a hush descended. She said, 'Today we are very fortunate.' She gestured to a man dressed as a soldier, his hair the same grey as their skirts, his face kind and strict. Mrs Gramm began to play 'All Things Bright and Beautiful' and they all stood up. They sang the song.

Afterwards the soldier asked them all to take a good long look out the window. He said, 'Some of your brothers and fathers are there. And there's no snow where they are.'

Then he asked them to lower their heads and pray and they did as they were told.

*

Miss Adams had never missed a Wednesday. Not for the dentist, not for the hairdresser; not when her sister from Vermont had finally come to visit. Not even when she sliced the tip of her left pinkie. Then she had been pale and digit-wrapped, but present nonetheless. So when Ruth's mother said, 'Honey, Miss Adams can't make it,' Ruth felt her tone was wrong. This was not clothes left on the floor, not what book was she reading.

'Why not?'

'I'm not sure. She didn't say. Probably she's busy. She teaches other girls, you know.'

'How many?'

'I don't know. Maybe five or six. Anyway, she'll be back next week. You can have a rest.'

She'd practised for nothing. Who'd hear it if not Miss Adams? Mom and Dad?

But no, she thought. It might be useful. There were fast passages, not as rapid as that opening drop, but still swift, and in one place, quite steep. Maybe she could borrow from them, find something to help.

On Wednesday morning they played rounders and she hurt her knee. After this Mr Matthews told them of the Great Depression. Carmen was sent to the office. In the afternoon they had a test Ruth didn't think she'd pass.

She was in the piano room when the clock struck six. She sat there until quarter past, a sick sensation ticking. Then she pretended that Miss Adams had asked. Ruth reached out, G sharp, F flat, fingers roaming, pressing out the notes. It moved in a stately fashion, occasionally darting forward, always settling back. And though it wasn't valleys, streams, at the end she did feel better. And it was as if the sounds had waited for her to finish: the front door shut, the mowers ran, dogs began to bark. She heard the stair creak, a carpet being beaten. She took the score from her bag.

She smoothed it over the Grieg. She lowered her hands. Then stopped. Because this was lesson time.

But there would be a week for it to fade (assuming Miss Adams was not too busy). So she bit her lip and started, and again she fell, early, badly, her foot-fingers twisted in the space between. She couldn't even listen to the Ashkenazy: his ease was someone running, laughing, shouting, look at *me*. Ruth wanted to tear it up, scatter and un-join its dots. But there was still the middle, its slow stream. It was like the answers in the back of the textbook: the problem was how to reach them.

*

Spring warmed into summer. Miss Adams returned, but now she only came every two weeks. And though she still spoke of Beginnings, she had new words too: *potential*; *promise*; *improvement*. Ruth blushed and just when she'd got used to this, when she started thinking, maybe she could ask, things came to an end. One day she got home and found that her mother had made her favourite.

After Ruth finished her mother said, 'Honey, I have good news.' And Ruth sat and listened, and although her mother saw her eyes moisten, she didn't see her cry. That happened ten minutes later, in the warm hug of her sheets. That Miss Adams was getting married, this was strange, she was the wrong age. But for her to move to Kansas, with a builder, this she could not accept.

That summer she read. She lay on the porch. She went to Church Youth Camp where someone almost drowned. She helped her mother. She followed the old train tracks until she got tired. And while she did these things, the dust on the piano smiled; began to feel settled.

The holidays ended. Leaves began to turn as breath began to smoke. Carmen said she'd had a boyfriend who had taken her to third base. Ruth's mother said she was having trouble finding a replacement. But she should practise anyway, go over some old pieces.

And so the dust was scattered, flung into a diaspora of the walls and corners. Ruth sat down with Liszt and Chopin, with Grieg and Debussy. One by one she propped them open, tried to play despite the quivering in her stomach. Although she made few mistakes, none of it felt right. She felt like something hollow that had been firmly struck.

She rested her hands on the keys. The sun entered the room. She pictured Miss Adams in Kansas, watching her husband build houses and saying *You began that well*.

Ruth pulled the score from the pile. She turned past the opening – even that brief glimpse produced a sense of vertigo – kept turning till she heard the river's liquid song. As she played the stream was chrome bright, silver scrawled on green. She wound with it through the valley, followed each meander. It was dizzying; she felt surrounded; wholly embraced by sound. When she finished, when the stream vanished, she began again.

Because – and she was sure of this – the main thing was to play. Miss Adams would never know. The slope could surely wait.

Vicki Husband

VIEW FROM THE NECROPOLIS

Laura and Annie arm in arm, a can each, meander through the stanes, the shrines, the domes like mosques, the tall crosses. Laura is mesmerised by the skyline bleeding from Rangers blue to the murky navy of her school uniform that she keeps at the back of her wardrobe. She's thinking about the show on Saturday and what she'll wear to the party after.

Annie's thinking about her nan. She lives in a place like this. Not as grand but. She visits it every year, takes her irises. When Annie was younger and acting up her mam would shout, 'Yir nan wud be turning in her grave.' It gave Annie the heebeegeebees to think of her nan, cold and stiff, rolling in the mucky earth. As she got older, it lost its effect. Although her mam would still say it if she thought Annie had taken a drink. Maybe cos Granda had been an alkie and both her nan and her mam were dead set against the drink. Laura's mam liked a swallie which meant Laura could lift a few cans fae her stash. Laura waited till her mam wis pished. It was easy then, like taking milk from a wain.

Annie looks at the view from the Necropolis and wonders if she has been further than she can see. The brewery chimneys aspire upwards, John Knox points an accusing finger at the sky – he gives her the creeps, the charred-looking cathedral stands behind him, the Royal Infirmary is a grim-looking pile at the rear and the Pinkston high flats spike the horizon like some bar-graph that she doesn't get. I can see yir flat, in fact I can see yir mam naked, Laura says. Where? says Annie mortified, laughing. That's no her boyfriend she's shagging – it's a burd, Laura ends herself on the grass; lies back gurgling, the lager foaming at the back of her throat.

Laura got picked for the show at the school. Annie didn't want to be in it; everyone's taking the piss out of it already before they've seen it. But Williams is organising the whole thing so Annie thinks it can't be that bad. They get Miss Williams for English and Annie likes the lessons, though she doesn't tell Laura. She and Laura sometimes pass the time by imagining what Williams' life is like: where she gets her clothes from, where she lives, what music she listens to, what she eats, who she shags. Laura quickly gets bored of this game, Annie doesn't but she feigns indifference. Laura is the talk of the school because she's the only second year to be in the show. She's got in with the fourth years from the chorus.

Annie thinks that she might go and see it for a laugh. She reckons that Laura hasn't got as much talent as she makes out but she's got something; she always gets chosen for stuff.

Annie won't lie on the grass cos she's got her Bench hoodie on that her mam got her yesterday and she'll kill her if it's dirty. Laura says she's no worried in her Goretex cos that's whit it's designed fir and so Annie pours a bit of lager o'er it tae see. Dinnae waste the can I've only got the four, Laura bellows. Mam wis crashed out after the game last night and the hoose wis dry so I had to beg my brother to buy me some and you know what a selfish bastard he can be. She jumps up, starts running, hair flinging out behind her; a clumsy comet orbiting the graves. Annie hides from her behind a stane and lights a spliff. Laura's no bothered about spliffs, says she prefers something to make her go faster, something that makes life brighter. Annie stares at the carvings on the graves a while, drinking it in. She loves auld stuff. It does her heid in thinking that the guy who carved it must be long deid; she traces the grooves of the lettering with her finger. Laura shrieks in her ear and she almost dies before chasing her to the bit where the cemetery ends and it slopes down to the back of the Tennent's factory.

Laura has stopped and is holding her finger to her mouth and pointing at the trees below. Annie can see the glow of a fag end and hears low voices circling it. Wylie's crew, Laura whispers. Bet they've got mair cans than us. Wylie's pal works in Tennent's that's where they get the pockle, Laura says. Annie knows that the workers get searched before they leave and so naebdy pockles from the factory; she knows cos her uncle used to work there but she doesn't argue. Laura says she can hear Marco's voice and Annie stops listening. Marco is the dark-haired boy from the year above. Laura says he's Italian but he speaks like he's fae Brigton. Annie thinks he's a tosser but there's nae talking to Laura about it, nae point falling oot o'er it. She watches as Laura stumbles down the dark path to the glow of light.

Annie wanders back up from the slope. She carves 'Laura and Annie' into green lichen on a stane and downs the last of her drink. She throws the can behind the railings of one of they small temples. It rattles against a pile of other offerings: faded cans, vodka bottles and milk cartons. It smells like a stank. The quiet falls about her. It's quite creepy but Annie likes it; that feeling you get watching a horror film. Annie loves horror films, they make her laugh. Laura is a wuss that way, she jist screams so you cannae hear the film, so it's no worth the rental. She'd watch them though, if a boy suggested it; says it's a guid excuse tae jump their bones.

Annie watches her breath form clouds in the freezing air. There is no way she's going down to Wylie's crew so she calls Laura, tells her she's going home. Coming, Laura's voice slurs on the mobile. Annie meets her at the top of the slope, she can hear the boys' voices louder now – rutting each other with rough boasts. Laura leans on Annie's arm half the way home. Laura's flat is empty though all the lights are on, and the telly. Annie manages to get her onto the bed and takes her trainers off. She only gets one arm out of the jacket before Laura slumps to the side so she'll just have to sleep in it. Annie walks the three blocks further on to her flat. Her Mam gives her an earful of abuse so she goes to her room to watch TV before falling asleep; she wakes up the next morning to some kids' programme way too loud.

*

When Laura died she was on page seven of the *Evening Times*. Annie knew that Laura would've bin ragin. She'd have expected front page and a picture but then she'd have to have bin mair inventive than jist a drugs overdose at fourteen to get a picture. Annie hadn't seen her fir six months since she'd starting hanging out wi Marco 24/7. Annie went to the funeral but she got annoyed at the fourth year lassies, who didn't even know Laura, bawling and greeting. She'd asked Williams how you went about getting buried in the Necropolis but it wis a no-go. Apparently it got filled up years ago. Dead rich and dead famous people are buried there and the rest. Williams had given her a book about it. The only book she'd read cover to cover. It smelt of her. She's seen Miss Williams out of school in her jeans and trainers, she seen her with another woman being close and that.

Annie went up to the Necropolis the week after the funeral, about the same time the two of them had been the year before. She found their names still there, where she'd scratched them and a few others added now beneath. She scratched deeper this time into the sandstone, it was soft enough for the key to bite in. She still had a T-shirt of Laura's that she'd borrowed and not given back so she burnt it, watched the embers die then kicked the ashes tae fuck around the grass. She opened a can fir old times' sake, though she rarely drunk lager now, and toasted Laura's borrowed gravestone.

The night tasted thick in her mouth; it tasted of the factory's sweet repulsive smell, of stale smoke, of buses revving and middens burning. It hung about her like fog. She wisnae scared though. She'd picked the night of an Old Firm game when she knew all the bampots would be in front of the box. She lay down on the ground, in her old hoodie, and looked at what would have bin the stars. Williams had done a poem wi the class about the stars and she'd explained that they were maistly dead. It blew Annie's mind so she looked it up on the internet when she got home. It said that the light from a star takes so long to reach us that by the time we see it, the star is maist likely dead. Like watching a film of an old Hollywood legend, Annie thought. Annie didn't want to be famous although she had auditioned for the show this year, she didn't get in. She wasn't sure what else she wanted to do. She'd told her mam that she loved English but Mam had said that English wasn't a job. She was still waiting for a boy to make a move on her; get it over and done with.

From where Annie lay, John Knox's finger appeared to hover, dismembered by the smog, pointing to the dead lights in the sky. The towers were pale shadows on the night behind him. She didnae bother about him this time, now that she knew he wasn't even buried here, it wis jist a statue. Williams' book had told her that. The infirmary windows looked warm almost inviting until Annie imagined the hunners of beds in there filled wi people moaning and groaning, knocked oot or dying. Some maybe lay on the operating tables right at that moment wi their intestines exposed; she pulled her sleeves down over her freezing fingers; a bit like a horror film withoot the laughs.

Annie lay still fir some time. She could feel the damp of the grass curling her hair. She was, she thought, waiting to be chosen for something; if she lay there long enough maybe she'd find out what fir. As she waited the ground grew uncomfortable, all lumps and bumps, and she wondered if it wis aw the bodies slowly turning the earth beneath her.

Elisabeth Ingram

GREEN LINE

The big white house nested absently on the scorched earth, a breezeblock box dropped light as trash by property developers out prospecting the empty hills. Even as the workers sweated into the earth and thrust down barbed steel prongs into sticky red gashes, they didn't look the house in the eye, their vision was so firmly fixed ahead, on the bare territory beyond that curved up into clean, green, untouchable mountains. Mountains so enticingly forbidden that the builders poured out their wet cement far too quickly, and built a wonky house.

To all eyes the house looked alien and temporary, shelved awkwardly, as if it was just about to flake off the scrubland in a scab of telegraph lines, paint and wires. The house bristled at the fringes, where prickly grasses matted up and tangled with the unfamiliar concrete block shade. Spiky clumps clenched around rocks, and scrunched down, chafing the soil. The bigger grasses all bowed down, perpetually poised to snap up silently, to flip the skew-whiff house off the face of the earth. When tepid retches of wet concrete had first rolled down onto the scorched orange soil, the spiky plants just shrugged, and sank down their grip into the ground. Snapping in half like lizard tails, they stretched down their roots deep into the earth, to shoot back up again around the foundations within a fortnight, giving the house the finger from all sides. The new tangles grew quickly, lushly and with pregnant girths, they huddled in corners and sent out parties to scatter and coil languorously around the concrete edges, and nonchalantly caress the walls with their barbs. Even the goats who herded by occasionally would jolt their bells into rattles as they stumbled around the house, falling off rocks.

Thirty years after the invasion, the soil around here is still so studded with land-mines that whole fields remain barb-wired with signs in those heavy Greek letters that stick out and trip up my British tongue. From this distance, the land inside the buffer zone looks exactly the same as the land outside. But each time the prospectors looked northwards they saw all the unexploded fields of the north. Fertile times before days lived in the south, before lines were drawn, and colours on a map ruled them into building new cities and a tourist industry from land that had only ever been used to grow potatoes. The white house sat in a wide bulge in the buffer zone, that everyone calls the Green Line. This strip of no-man's-land veins through the centre of the island and ranges in width from a few metres, to hundreds of kilometres, and is not green at all. Denied to them entirely, all the men desired the prohibited land all the more, and the craving to cut the vein open increased until they had to leave. The prospectors stripped the olive trees bare before dawn one day, and stopped gashing jealous grey tarmac strips all over the hills. They followed the dry river bed back down the hill to the golden seafront sands to flashier attractions, to build Olympic-size hotel pools and swim in easier money.

I live here now. We retired here, our cut-price place in the sun. My single house is surrounded by nothing but dust, rocks and breeze, and a dense grid of unfinished roads that don't connect to any actual roads or lead to any actual places. Except for my plot, the driveways all lead to scrubby soil, and rocks that scatter watchful reptiles at the sound of my footsteps. I could walk off whole days around the hills using only these webs of tarmac lines and meet only snake tracks and paw prints. Pink-flowering bushes grow all day and all night in the glow of the occasional lamppost, where the entire width of the road is swallowed and shimmers electric in a green and pink burst of astonishment at this connection to the power grid. Giant engorged flowers quiver as you brush by, and spit yellow pollen in your face.

The lightning spikes came at the end of the summer, and the wind set fire to the pine trees in the hills above the house. In the Green Line, rain soaked into the blue berets of UN peacekeepers. If I climb on the roof of my house, I can see them in their towers, and the matchbox-size sickle moon carved into the mountains far off in the north, which blushes cherry red after a downpour in the hills. Unfolding rounds of cloudbursts tested the ground around the barbed wire, and then evaporated as quickly as they came, pulling soil through the house in burning gold coughs and sneezes, leaving a sickly dryness that hovered over everything, shifting thickly. Everything was exhaling. The storms took months to shake off. Except for briefly blinking open the doors to sweep out dust, I closed up the house during these daytime windstorms, and, as if the wind was afraid of the dark, with each night came stillness. In the day, I was contained. As sealed up and shut in to the dust as an eyeball, stirring under a tight white eyelid. Shut in from the dirt, I maintained the order of the house, and it remained very still on the hill, this summer. Sometimes, I can still hear the outside, feel it, ache it even, as its dust knots my lungs and crunches between my teeth. Inside, it is still and clean, and the sky is a muffled noise, and the earth is a quiet taste in my mouth.

Far away the prospectors are strengthening and regrouping. Their yellow machinery is digging up the distance, and the multiplying sprawl of tiny red scattered lumps is spreading into an angry raised patch of terracotta roof tiles. Where once there was clean land, now white dots and glass glints swell the landscape like honey bee stings, each hotel and holiday home releasing pheromones that call all the other bees to sting the ground, too. When the builders stuck in, and started digging at the bottom of my hill, I knew that I had to leave.

It should be easy to pack up and go: everything is contained here. Ten feet around the house runs a kneecap-high white breezeblock wall, which contains the same hot dry brush as surrounds it. Not much else – an empty steel-barred dog cage, with sun on all sides, where occasionally tiny brown birds sniff a captive scent, and tease the padlocks by swooping into the cage and flying right back out again through the other side. A traditional outdoor bread oven cooks in the heat, empty. And then there is the grey steel storage building. Twice as long as the house itself, and half as wide, with corrugated funnels that the sun runs down twice a day to check for shadows. With no windows, the air must be hot and dark inside: tin-canned air. The light keeps bouncing off the steel, into my eyes, heating the sealed innards which are locked up tight and filled with unpacked boxes.

It has been easy to pack up the house; we have lived here for years without ever unpacking most of the boxes we shipped over from England. Today, my home is empty, and the men are outside, lifting heavy boxes, moving us out. Out of my house, which was white, inside and out, and had gold taps which ran cold water for hours. The floors were grey-veined white marble. No people came by. When a praying mantis came in, I opened a window, and the next day he was gone. The same with a snake this summer – a small brown line – he left, through the open back door, pushing off the frame with a flick-*ik* of distaste. What little passed directly by me hardly paused to cool its skin. We were treading so softly on the ground, that when the black cracks in the white plaster appeared last spring, I touched them and welcomed them as a sign that perhaps now, finally, the house was settling down.

Even during the windstorms, I always spent dusk on my small bedroom terrace, where I hovered lightly above the ground, pinning fabric into a wooden hoop and embroidering in the gold-dipped light, as it cooled to silver. I would stop my stitches with the dimming light to watch the night sky, the deepening blue and the dimming glow. My heart felt old, waiting so far away for the stars to appear. I cricked my neck for Venus, aligned myself with the cloudy Milky Way, and watched, as the satellites slid around me steady in their groove. By the early morning breaths, when the silver dots evaporated into one cool pool, and the steel needle threaded in my fingers was sharp to my eyes again, I would stitch a few last stars. I would embroider that past night, its slow lights and half lights, directly into my dark cloths, as gently as the stars themselves had appeared. And when the sky grew too white, and the winds pulled up the heat and dust again, I'd move inside and let the sands rub away the day.

I'd clean the marble floors, the stairs, the walls and doors, both upstairs and down, wiping the wood and the stone with a wet cloth and a dry brush, sweeping out the dusty amber frost that somehow still blew in each and every day through the nooks and the cracks. I had not seen you much since we fought, so I was alone. I liked it. The wind and sometimes the rain would hum and drone me to sleep in the afternoon, a solid necessary noise, like an aircraft engine. As the wind fell, I would wake with the absence of noise, and start out of my bed. I'd fetch water from a blue plastic canister, and pour it into a glass with three ice-cubes. Then I'd head outside again to my terrace in the sky, and sit, and sip, and tap the condensation from the glass to my fingers, down onto my face like rain.

The embroidery was large by now, as finished and unfinished as the sky. Every night and every morning I felt I had watched and worked more intensely, and with more precision, than the night before, fixing the night sky onto the dark cloths with sparkling silk threads. I had returned to the fabric each evening until it became sedimented and tough. There were no new stars appearing, and no new galaxies unfolding. The sky sank deeper each day and only the texture of the night changed. It was so dense, I could run my fingernail along it and I would bump into silver stars like gravel on a road, crashing over the night in a scratch. I could feel each star's skeleton. I so wanted to capture the stars for you, to let you know that I do love you. I wanted to lay my dreams under your feet like my favourite poem.

When you moved in, my teenage sons moved out to give you space. It has been fifteen years since you all bumped boxes in that Manchester hallway, and we stacked your belongings in the living room. You had accumulated so many odd things during your first marriage it astounded me, I peeped in on your past, at your dog whistles inaudible to the human ear, your two identical pairs of white patent shoes and the leather trousers with snakeskin patches, and those empty plastic yoghurt pots you like to keep 'for storage'. You sat these things in piles, then more things came along, which sat in towers, on top of boxes, full of other things. When the towers started crashing over and leaving trails of mismatched broken ceramics and strange dried powders and sticky stains, I began to put the towers back in the boxes. You just made more towers, and then I filled more boxes. It was what we did for a while, until I asked you to spring-clean, and you left.

When you came home again, half-empty boxes and piles of junk began to accumulate in the strangest places – inside the shower cubicle and bathtub, underneath the kitchen table, on top of, in front of, and finally inside of our wardrobe. In the beginning we left a bed and a narrow route for guests to reach it, through an aisle of boxes, but then boxes crept onto the bed too, and soon the boxes reached to the ceiling, and the only way to deal them was to shut the door.

You snarled and watched your feet as I drove to the industrial estate and piled up box after box into the storage unit. When I had finished, and the storage unit was ready to shut for the day, you unstacked them all, and restacked them again in a different order, placing down each box as gently as a newborn into its mothers arms. The caretaker kept hawking up snot and spitting it on the ground.

When we retired to Greece, the boxes came with us. They arrived late, after eight months in a shipping container, at which point we moved to a bigger house to accommodate them. We needed somewhere with enough room, and you decided unpacking would be futile until we settled on the right house. The houses did get bigger each time, mainly because of the photographs. There were nine cameras (which you never kept in a box), and at first I had just thought they were another collection, a pile, like everything else, simply because they sat on the shelf along with your collections of paintbrushes and forty-eight daylight light bulbs. Apparently each brand of light bulb has a different quality of light.

When we moved the last time, to house number seven, I continued the lease on number six too, so we had a place to keep your boxes: so we wouldn't have to move them again. You took to visiting number six every day, and called this 'going to the office'. You filled the house upstairs and down in less than six months, and the overflow came to our new house with the corrugated-steel hangar in the garden, built to house boats in the winter. You put floor-to-ceiling boxes in there, and sealed them in the heat.

Now, you say you don't want to move house ever again. Last month, for the first time in thirty years it became possible for people to cross the Green Line from both sides, and the country has more freedom and signs of political progress since the 1970s. There is a whole side of the country we have never seen. This leap towards unification has also been marked by prospectors circling our house more intently, more landing each week, the swarm protecting their hive. The problem is they sting the soil, and they hook their barbs in so deep that they can't tear themselves away. More follow and sting and protect and swell and litter the land until it's so unrecognisably deformed with development that it's buzzing with death rattles.

You argue you want to stay here for ever, to watch television as the builders hover over more and more fields and draw more and more lines around us dividing up the land until we live in a scribble. Living in a ceasefire line full of crickets and starlight and empty days was fine, but now I'm waking up to machines tearing swimming pools into the ground, and revving and reversing with alarms that beep-beep-beep-beep backwards, then rev to the front, and beep to the back again, vehicles tearing up the ground and honking out warnings day and night. You want to stay here, with me and a house and a shed full of boxes, buffered by a lawn with a water sprinkler and pink roses pissed on by a small mean poodle that yaps whenever I leave the house.

This is your last stand, I suppose. When I heard your car engine leave this morning, I stepped into the garden to unlock the steel doors and found every single box still in there, untouched. You went into the corrugated shed each day this past fortnight, I heard you come and go from inside my shuttered house, but it seems you just slammed in, and out. You sat there, in the dark, sweating a plan to make me stay. Reinforcing your cardboard blockade. And I folded. I did go straight back inside today and I did phone the shipping company and, yes, I did pay an absurdly enormous last-minute excess fee to ship home all of your boxes, and not just the twenty that we had agreed on a month ago, before you went to live in the office for four stormy weeks, leaving me with all this silence. And in the dirt and the white heat of day, when I should be wiping down the cool marble for a last time, brushing out the orange dust, waiting for the daylight to drip to gold and a taxi horn to honk, I am zipping my knife along packing tape, and opening up your boxes.

The first I cut open is full of empty white yoghurt pots. A box full of nothing, plastic and air shunted around from dark rooms to sheds to garages, across oceans, countries and years. The second box I knife is white, pristine and as undented as when you filled it full of photographs of kittens, cars, street signs and strangers ten years ago. These are the exact same boxes we packed up and shipped to Greece so many moons ago. They have been sitting, untouched, unopened ever since, years, sealed in the dark.

In the bright light of noon I step back inside the house to turn off the power, finish up, lock up, fetch my bags, say goodbye. I sit outside on the breezeblock wall, and press the embroidery to my mouth. I snap a single silk thread with my teeth. With my incisors, I grip and pull, and unravel a star to black. It had taken me weeks to embroider the dimpled moon. I snap it, all of it, and pull out every glinting thread until my gums bleed metallic juices. I am packing up the moon and dismantling the sun and spitting out sparking metallic froths. The holes in the dark cloth are Braille to my fingers, and the fallen stars just fizz away into zeros, bare, clean, honest air. I lay the threadbare cloth down on the earth, where the wind throws it up and ensnares it in an olive tree. The cloth flops down thinly, exhaling and inhaling irregularly with the tree, slapping back softly at the wind.

Now, the wind has risen further, and the two dump trucks I ordered are crushing each box we own into tiny scrambled pieces. Your boxes creak before they fold in on themselves and your yoghurt pots pop.

I can't watch. I'm listening to the crumps and snaps, curled up in the hot dark, feeling the corrugated fibres against my face, waiting for my turn. You will come home and see my embroidery for the first time, ripped apart and hyperventilating in the olive tree. You'll walk up to it, look up and see the bright hot daylight shooting through each pinprick, the white light piercing the black fabric into an open starscape, a cloth infused with an exact reflection of the night. You will see the bare unburdened cloths of heaven, and you will see that they are full of holes. You will either see nothing at all, or you will see my cloth, enwrought with light, and laid out before you, studded and weighty with punctures.

Kirstin Innes

COUNTRY DANCING 1994
an excerpt from *Dance Me In*

What is the *point*, they all whisper to each other.
The teachers said
ah, you'll all need a wee refresher before the Christmas dance, eh!
but they'd actually got in a DJ for the Christmas
dance, which they were actually having in the upstairs room of
that M8 nightclub this year and Karen Fyfe had actually not got
KBd by the bouncers there last week – although a hissed, high-
pitched rumour said it was just because her mum was shagging
the owner –
but anyway but ANYWAY shut up, right, cos that's
hows we got it for the dance in the first place and Laura White's got
a gold body she's wearing with they new white jeans –
as the goth
kids scowled and rolled their eyes at this, Kate Dey peeling the
laces slo-o-owly out of her Docs –
WILL YOU COME ON GIRLS.
The odd giggle breaks rank and Mzz Reynolds you have to remember
not to call her Mrs Doubal any more shoots it down with a whipcrack look
because her face was much harder this term –
fuck her anyway soor auld cow, not surprised her man left her –
but really you're too busy adjusting your
bra so the padding doesn't stick out or pulling up your shorts
or sticking your fingers in the corners of your eyes for blobs of
mascara or whispering to Emma Faulkes *how does my hair look, is
it okay –*
because in eight seconds Mrs Doubal would open the
door and you would all file into the Hall, which still smelled of old
sweat and rubber and the rotted bits off of those sashes they made
you wear for basketball, and you would go and find seats on the
benches along the wall and a door on the other side would open
and in would come the BOYS.

What is the *point*, they all whisper to each other.
Staring straight ahead, not looking at each other as you change
cos you don't want to be called a *gay* and you don't even want
to see other boys' dicks, anyway, not even just to check. James

Gibson picks up Daniel Hopkins' crap trainers, holds them above his head till he gets bored cos no-one's laughing today. The pressed washing powder of gym kit mingles with sour rank fart stink and somebody cackles *ya manky basturt* –
                          Mr Collins? How comes we have to do this again? We're not even having a ceilidh at our Christmas dance this year –
   Well Steven, you'll use these dances as adults. These are important skills you're learning.
                          but we already know them, sir –
                          yeah, we've done them for years –
                          yeah, we started doing them in PRIMARY, sir –
Mr Collins doesn't answer, just chuckles and wanders off.
                                          Hurry up there, boys.
Still, you couldn't help but notice that there were less skivers than usual PE classes. Not as many girls bringing in notes from their mums written in Katy Cooper's left hand on snipped jotter paper in the back of maths, staring nervy wee Mr Henderson straight in the eyes and saying WOMEN'S TROUBLE.
   Not as many boys just not turning up at all.

Fucking look at Emma Faulkes's tits in that T-shirt, bet you she's not even wearing a bra ohoho bet you I can make her bounce –
                          m o s t l y,
though, the boys are quiet because country dancing was reeeeally fuckin embarrassin so everybody hears James Gibson above the scuffling as you sit. Emma Faulkes shouting *as if ya wee ginger scrote!* across the hall but going pure red and crossing her arms over her chest anyway, *total* beamer –
                          Mr Collins, sensing trouble thirty seconds too late as ever, wanders over with his neck out like a giraffe in glasses saying
                          what's the trouble here?
Mr Collins, who called his wife his **partner** when he had you for Guidance; who would be found in his car in your sixth year with a hosepipe through the window.

It wasn't until Mr Henderson had the bright idea of putting the tape player on to shut everyone up, all those fuzzy, creaky old bagpipes or whatever they were playing the first **Chord** and he and Mzzz Reynolds actually bowing to each other *ohmyGOD* that you all remembered, like you did ever year, that Country Dancing?

Was for fannies.

Right Everybody! It's been a year, and you might not remember these, so we're going to start you off with a nice easy one:

Gordon Fox and Nora Gordon, although they don't know it, both reciting the same litany under their breath: please not the please not the please not the

it's the Gay Gordons!

On the boys' benches: *WOOHOO! Hiya Gordon!*

James Gibson and Stevie Paterson doing bendy wrists –
On the girls' benches: *Zat true, is it Nora?*

Big Kelly Anderson hissing *Fucking lezzer. Fucking better not get anywhere near ME. Aye, she was totally looking at your tits in the changing room, Kelly, so she was,* wee keen nippy Karen Fyfe who you hated, bet it was true about her mum, too –

Nora and Gordon both keep looking at the floor, would bump into each other at forty-two when Nora was picketing the lawyer's office Gordon worked at, avoid each other's eyes for the self-same reason.

Mr Collins, ineffectual as nothingness:

QUIETEN DOWN THERE –

Chord.

Mr Henderson and Mrs Do–Mzz Reynolds bow to each other again, oh god and the fiddles start up yeah, you had all forgotten about the fiddles. Mr Henderson and Mzz Reynolds hold each other's hands as far away from each other as possible, Mzzz Reynolds doing that embarrassing dance teacher thing where she tried to point her toes in trainers, sad, sad eyes.

Stevie Paterson wolfwhistled.

Dee-edle deedle deedle deedle dee dee dee!
AND a-one two three TURN back two three,

Sheree Robertson and Fiona Donaldson sitting beside each other both eyeing the wall above Ryan Woodbridge's head. Ryan, the only boy too cool to change out of his Docs and skinny jeans for it. Ryan with his stoned grin and his Mohawk, and his beautiful, soulful eyes –

Sheree and Ryan in a bar, both twenty-nine, after he messaged her on Facebook. He almost wouldn't recognise her in the suit and she almost wouldn't recognise him with the beard, and having never spoken at school they wouldn't have very much to say to each other until the drink kicked in, by which time they were too pissed for the sex to be any good, and she'd leave before he woke, embarrassed.

FORWARD two three and back two three
Elaine McKenzie flutters her fingers across the hall to Ally Kelly and he grins back, although he looks a bit embarrassed and Laura White whispers to Laura Lyle – they *totally* actually DID it last week and *actually* she thinks she's pregnant because even though it went soft she said there was a bit of wet stuff on the end of it –

And SPIN. And SPIN. And SPIN. And SPIN.
Just the ladies spin, remember, third year. Not the gentlemen!
And polKA polKA polKA polKA polKA polKA!
Stevie Paterson whispered to Fraser Green that Ally Kelly totally RODE Elaine McKenzie last week and Fraser Green went pure red, *total* beamer, and hoped he wouldn't get hard –
                                              he was getting hard.
He was getting hard and the music had stopped and they were about to make them stand up oh shit –
Okay third year! Anyone need to see that again?
– no, I don't think you do, Mister Gibson –
Al-RIGHT, everyone into the centre and take your
partners for the
                        don't say it again don't say it again *please*
Gay Gordons!

And you cluster together, looking at walls and shoes and the scabby football goals taped on the floor, and all the proper long-term couples like Ally Kelly and Elaine McKenzie, Paul Hume and Susan White, Katy Cooper and Calum Auld pair off silently and are co-opted into the big invisible circle that only Mr Henderson could see –
                        and then there is the awful bit where nobody speaks. Five girls stare hopefully at Chris Wood who is *gorgeous*, picks Karen Fyfe *Karen FYFE*? and Mr Collins says something hearty and awful like every year –
I'm going to have to pair you off myself if you don't get
cracking, third year! Would have thought you were too
old for this by now!

and this meant you could go with a boy or a girl who you were friends with a bit, now, so that was all right –

> Craig Thomas and Anna Wylie
>
> Sarah Irvine and Ben Parnell
>
> Ryan Woodbridge.
>
> Ryan Woodbridge.

Ryan Woodbridge is asking Samira Mesbah.

And then you notice it's getting scarce and you just have to ask ANYBODY because nobody wants to get left with Rosemary Stewart with her scabby face and her big posh voice answering all the maths questions right, or wee smelly Philip Forrest who got a hard-on watching Lynsey McGovern in the pool that time in first year. Those two end up dancing together just like they always do –

oohHOOH! Got yourself a hot one there, eh Philly?

Rosemary Stewart grew elephant skin, ignored the catcalls, headed straight for Pure Maths at Cambridge, where people with big posh voices like her would never quite take her to their hearts and she hoped, when she gave it any thought at all, that it was just because she had gone to a state school –

Everyone into the circle, now. Settle DOWN, third year! Chord.

The skipping and the turning comes naturally now because you've danced this dance twice a week every December since you were eight. It lies there in you, seeps back through your skin at the weirdest times, usually at weddings. Autopilot. At Sarah Irvine's, her new English husband's sister will ask you to show her the dances by way of asking you to sleep with her, and you'll grin and explain her through the Gay Gordons, hamming up the accent, saying that ach, it was practically whipped into you at school, this is the closest to a race memory that oor generation's got and you'll laugh, pull her close for the **polKA polKA polKA** bit –

but for now EMMA FAULKES'S ACTUAL TITS are right beside you and you're going to get hard again, you know you are –

until James Gibson pushes Fiona Donaldson off him and goes EW you just farted! and everyone stops and laughs and Fiona Donaldson runs off through the girls' door with Mrs Doubal after her and the music carries on on the tape, **deedle deedle deedle** while Mr Collins marches James Gibson out through the boys' with a finger behind his scarlet ear, as red as his hair –

Carry on, third year!
                                    and BACK two three
four nerdy NERDY wee Daniel Hopkins *actually* counting under
his breath can't *believe* you have to dance with him just don't look
and it'll be over soon –
                        and FORWARD two three four as Paul
Brown's meaty fat arms are turning tiny Michelle Shek who looks
like a bird (will get pregnant and drop out before the Standard
Grades). Paul Brown (the first of the year to die, heart attack after
too much coke aged twenty-three, you heard) hisses, *Just because I
asked you to dance doesn't mean I fancy you, right* –
                                    AS IF, Michelle says back.
I've got a boyfriend at St Tams anyway –
                                    both of them lying –
                                                        and
SPIN and SPIN and Nora Gordon is getting pissed off with
the way lanky stupid Ian Christie just STANDS there when he's
supposed to be twirling her, wonders why it HAS to be girl/
stupidboy partners anyway, stupid homophobic school system,
looks shyly over his stupid arm at Alice Armstrong, whose lips
taste of White Lightning were sweet and cold behind a tree when
you were both coming back from the shop to the benches with
more cider on Saturday night –
                        and polKA polKA Stevie Paterson
is suddenly laughing and driving you straight into John Wilson and
Heather Kilpatrick ahead of you, and he's shouting *PILE ON* –
                                                        and
they all fall over, Mzzz Reynolds running straight in to the centre,
not speaking, just blowing her whistle for ages as the tape does a
final –
                                    Chord.
and you all let go of each other's hands.

                        Immediately.

Mary Johnston

GOWSTIE GABERLUNZIE

Late ae mugglie November nicht I met a gaberlunzie,
breweries bruised barley braith writhin up the closes,
topaz glimmerin street lichts blintered doon throu the mirk
on hameless loons wi 'Carlies' handin roon a spliff,
New Age gaberlunzies, shargart, shilpit loons
in foosty aal deen anoraks, maakin for the nicht.

Like a blue-gooned-badged King's Bedesman,
he loomed oot o the smaa-weet nicht,
his back stracht an stechie, he cam shachlin
up the street, his face wizzent, peelie-wally,
grey yim on his dowie een, a snaa fite pow,
hans raxed oot, a gaberlunzie frae time afore.

I gie him a bit fite siller, he taks hud o baith ma hans,
I've nae notion ti be toucht bi him but he lays
his face gainst mine: I smell cald caller air on him,
nae alcohol, nae foost, like faither's beardie fen a bairn
grey stibble scrapes ma chin, syne letting go ma hans,
he says, *God bless you miss, God bless.*

I met a gaberlunzie ae mugglie November nicht,
ill-eesed, puir an hameless, ma charitie he blesst.

*In Scotland in the 17th and 18th centuries beggars were licensed; they
wore blue gowns with badges and were known as the King's Bedesmen.
In return they were to offer daily prayers for the King and his Court.*

Bridget Khursheed

THE FISH LADDER

A toddler's walk to the lake's edge
and its two bridges hugging the shore;
a freshwater beach and low wall
ideal for my son to splash in;
there's nothing wrong here.

Just the bluish cushions of water
piled like a child's game to avoid:
the current's fast; no ladder
but a conveyor belt of lust,
Rapunzel's hair skeining over.

This thing must happen.
Milt and roe on the gravel
and smolt, fragile as ice, sharding
down the river to the sea.
This place not memorable is known:

salmon die for a second sight.
Rucksacked, the baby cries for home.
We climb, all snacks gone,
to a rented cottage and maps.
I don't think I'll get back.

Eleanor Livingstone

NOVA SCOTIA?

He's fat, bald, mid fifties, with a short beard
and earrings, exudes an air of menace
nicely wrapped. *Aw right if I sit here?*
He winks, and the guard blows her whistle.
It's August, festival time. He and I
have both left venues where others are still
enjoying an evening out beneath the red glow
of heaters warming up our northern sky.

From a Marks and Spencer's carrier bag
he offers smoked salmon and *a soft
little Chardonnay – hail the rotten fruit!*
– if I don't mind drinking from the bottle.
He's going home to Dundee. *Aberdeen?
Even seagulls can't afford to eat there.*

BREATHLESS

Beyond ruined houses and a past
eroded by salt and marram grass
stretch miles of sand dunes
where as kids we hurled ourselves
into space, legs and rebel cries
suspended in the air, landing

spread-eagled in cotton shorts
and bare legs, winded but alive.

On August evenings years later
under cover of dark we returned
stumbling in and out of rabbit holes
to find the sand sun-warmed, soft
and far enough removed for us
to lie as still and silent as the sea

but for fingers finding buttons
and the racket of our hearts.

Rowena M. Love

GUTTER GIRL

Shoals of photos swam round the walls
in the cold hall where I met you first.
I was drowning in picture after picture
of a Shetland long ago, when you hooked me out.

Four happy lasses round a barrel,
hands and aprons bloodied with your work
(black and white no barrier to the red).
Behind you, like waves preserved forever,
row upon row of barrels salted with herring
you'd gutted and packed; a bristle of masts.
Your smile not the bait, bright though it was,
but the caption. Four girls, only three names.

You don't seem stern, or different from the rest,
so why does no one know who you were?
Was there a falling out over a fisherman
more muscled than the rest or with a tongue slick as fish?
Did tragedy fillet your friendship,
leaving it raw and unhealed?
Or had you just had enough of herring,
settled for a farm boy from home?

Later, in Lerwick, we followed the lure
of live music to *Da Noost*. Fiddle and squeezebox
transformed pokey pub into hub of activity;
delight rising from the smoke
like Brigadoon from mist,
tinted with whisky and toe-tapping rhythm.

Surveying the crowded swell, that flowed
to the bar and back or swayed in their seats to the music,
my eye caught your picture on the wall.
Same photo, different frame. No captions at *Da Noost*,
but I knew your name was still missing.
Your presence, its absence
swallowed, hollowed the laughter.
All evening, my gaze sought you out
like tongue to a sore tooth.

Back home, I netted Shetland museum online;
found you cached there, waiting for me.
Downloaded you to my computer to stare at,
print off and pin to my wall, invent stories about.
Your voice in my head, husky as skua.
Your hands rough as herring gills
from your work; they snag my peace of mind.
You fade like a photo left in sun,
until the next time I trace your passing
from scales you left glistening in your wake.

Harry McDonald

ALZHEIMER'S

Most days
Her mood was
Like broken glass.

The splintered edges
Of what had once been whole
Were all that remained.

Each morning,
In an ancient ceremony,
He took her tea
Brewed amber

And equilateral triangles
Toasted golden, with
A skin of yellow butter
On one side.

Anchored at a safe distance,
I ask him why he
Repeats this dawn ritual.

He blinked at me,
Ship to ship,
Foolish child.

I saw then,
Her disease
Reflected in his face,
Its image scattered
As in a shattered mirror.

*When she comes back
I want to be here,*
Was all that he said.

Joe McInnes

HEARTLINES

Young Chaz Malloy looked beautiful. He sauntered along the street in his mother's beautiful summer dress. He wished she was here to see him. She'd not been seen since spring. Disappeared on a cold March morning, departing with a promise of return.

Across on the spare ground, Brian Cassidy and his mates were running round mad, playing football. It was the middle of August and the street teemed with children revelling in the summer heat. Chaz had almost turned the corner when the sound of his father Old Man Malloy's voice came hollering over the big blue veranda.

'Chaz Malloy, ya crazy bastard, jist what the hell dae ye think yer playing at?' He was half naked and woken up off a night-shift. His bawling drew the attention of the other kids.

'Check out crazy Chaz,' yelled Brian Cassidy, scooping up his football and making a dash toward the boy in the dress. The rest of his team followed.

'Gie's a kiss, Chaz Malloy,' Brian shouted in Chaz's face, grabbing a hold of his wrist.

Young Chaz Malloy, who'd grown up in these same streets, puckered his red-lipstick-lips and pouted, 'You can call me Charlene.'

'Fuck you, ya pervert,' shrieked a disgusted Brian.

Chaz twirled, curtsied, wriggled his arse. 'If wishes wur kisses.'

'Get up these sterrs afore I come doon ther an wring yer neck,' fumed Old Man Malloy, his knuckles gripped tight on the blue veranda, the only thing saving him jumping over three flights.

Every kid in the street abandoned their game, eager not to miss out on the freak show.

'Show's yer knickers, Chaz,' shouted Anne Black. 'Gie's a squeeze ae yer tits.'

Chaz lifted up his dress. 'I've no gote any tits, but yer welcome tae a feel ae ma fanny.'

'When I get ma hauns oan you I'm gonnae throttle ye,' roared Old Man Malloy, disappearing behind the porch.

Chaz ran like fuck, high heels clattering along the pavement. Old Man Malloy came tearing out the close in his Y-fronts. Chaz pulled off his stilettos, hiked his dress over his knees and bolted through a close mouth into the back court, the feel of grass under his feet spurring him forward. He jumped over the fence into the next back, side-stepping the washing hanging on the clothes line.

Old Man Malloy: 'I shoulda droont ye at birth, ya crazy bastard.'

But that didn't stop Chaz, he hot-footed it through the back green like Shergar in a frock. Eventually he came to a stop a few streets up the block and rested beneath the windows. Gasping with exhaustion he looked across a horde of pebble-grey buildings where a sea of blue verandas fluttered like banners in the August heat. As if someone had planned a mass demonstration and the people had refused to come.

Chaz was in shit street. There was a huge tear down one side of his mother's dress. He considered ripping the other side as a fashion statement, but decided the one slash looked pretty chic. Catching his reflection on a window he noticed his lipstick spread all across his chin. He fixed his face and pulled the loose threads from his dress.

'Chaz Malloy, ur ye some kind ae pervert? What ye doin peeking in that bedroom windae?' Jamie Gallagher leaning out a back window. The house was on the ground floor and Jamie jumped out the window and crossed over the back. 'Is that lipstick yer wearen?'

'It's ma Ma's.'

'Ye've gote it smeared ourr yer cheeks like a blusher,' said Jamie, drawing a finger across Chaz's face. 'Ye look like a clown.' He grabbed hold of the hem of the dress, spat on it, and scoured Max Factor off Chaz's ruddy cheeks.

'So wer ye aff tae awe dressed up?'

'Ourr the burn tae collect flowers fur ma Ma.'

'I'm watchen ma wee sister,' said Jamie. 'Or else I'd huv come wi ye.'

'I'll pick ye sum love-me-nots.'

'I better get back ourr the house,' said Jamie, and vaulted over the fence.

Chaz strolled through the backs in his bare feet, his mother's high heels swinging from his fingers. He arrived at the edge of the housing scheme. The field across the road led toward the burn. He crossed over onto the soft grass where doocots stood guard like massive crows.

Chaz was thirsty. But he knew enough not to drink burn water. His mother Sabby Malloy had warned him, 'If ye drink burn water yer tongue wull turn blue, but that won't matter cos ye won't be able to see it if yer blind.' Instead of drinking the water

Chaz decided to go for a paddle. He didn't have to take off socks
or untie shoelaces, or roll up his trouser legs, but simply slipped on
the high heels, lifted his dress and stepped into the stream. Even
in summer the water was cold and stones cut into his feet. After a
while he got used to numb feet and began to enjoy the sensation of
the water swirling around his legs. He let go his hold on the dress
and it floated on the surface of the river. Water splashed against
his thighs.

'Ye better be careful ye don't fall under.' A voice by the edge
of the burn.

There was a man stood on the river bank, wearing a dark blue
boiler suit tied at the waist, and a T-shirt of the same colour. Chaz
recognized the clothes of a worker from one of the nearby factories.
Only this workman was leaning on a long piece of stick, almost as
tall as himself. He was smiling.

'Yer dress wull get soaked.'

'It's no ma dress,' said Chaz, swishing his fingers against the
flow of current, becoming conscious again of the chill on his legs.
Water lapped over the bottom of the dress and it dragged beneath
the surface. The man leant over the edge of the river and stretched
out the stick, offering it for Chaz to grab on to. Chaz took a
hold on it and waded toward the bank. When he stepped out the
burn one of his shoes was missing and his foot got caked in mud
scrambling up the embankment.

'Ye've ripped yer dress.'

Chaz tugged the torn dress across his legs. It was wet and stuck
to his thighs. 'It's no ma dress,' he persisted, hanging his legs over
the edge of the burn, pulling on a tuft of grass to wipe his foot.
'I like yer stick, did ye make it yersel?' he added, trying to change
the subject.

The man looked at the piece of wood as if regarding it for the
first time. 'It's only a branch ae hawthorn, I found it in the wids an
scraped aff the bark, gied it a rub doon wi sandpaper.'

'It's a good pattern. How dae ye get the lines runnen throu
it?'

'That's jist natural,' replied the man. 'It's the grain, awe wid
has a grain.'

'But that looks a special design.'

'I rubbed linseed oil intae the wid tae bring out the grain. I
gote it out the work, the linseed oil.'

'It looks pure magic,' said Chaz.

'If yer interested I could show ye how different wid has
different patterns. Awe ye need tae dae is peel aff the bark. If ye

come intae the wids I'll strip doon that silver birch tree. Cut intae its heartline.'

'What's a heartline?'

'Come ourr tae the wids an I'll show ye.'

'I need tae wait here fur ma Da,' replied Chaz. 'He's up at his doocot, he telt me no tae move from here. He shouldnae be long.'

'I'll tell ye what, come intae the wids an I'll gie ye the stick tae keep.'

Chaz searched the empty sky for tumbling birds as the man led him over toward the trees. Handing him the hawthorn staff the man pulled a knife from his pocket and began to skin the bark off a birch tree.

'The centre ae every tree has a heart grain,' he explained. 'The lines oan the pattern ae the heart grain ur called heartlines.'

Sap oozed from the trunk of the tree and leaked across the man's fingers as he meticulously stroked the blade across the exposed birch wood.

His mother Sabby Malloy once told Chaz trees were just like living creatures. They could feel things just like human beings. If you hurt them they scream. Chaz imagined he could hear the birch tree screaming as the man hacked into its heartline.

'Did ye hear someten?' The man stopped, his face dripping with sweat as he pulled his knife out the broken tree.

The wood was silent.

Chaz wanted to go home. He wanted to be out in the street playing football. He wanted to put his clothes back on.

The man scanned the trees for movement. His eyes flitting through the thicket came to rest on a juniper tree. Chaz followed the line of his gaze across the woodland. At first all he could see was the reddish juniper bush, and then slowly, he began to make out the outline of an animal. He couldn't tell who was first to move, the deer or the man. The deer ran straight towards them and the man scrambled backward, as if he could hardly believe it. Just as the deer was upon them it swerved sideward, kicking fallen leaf off the forest floor, scampering off through the undergrowth, almost brushing Chaz as it bounded by.

The man regained his footing and careered through the wood in pursuit.

Chaz stood there, still gripping the hawthorn staff, the bark from the silver birch discarded at his feet. He looked on the gaping wound of the tree, but instead of a heartline the core of the tree was rotting. In that moment Chaz realized his mother was wrong.

Trees don't scream. Trees don't feel things like human beings. And he knew also, as the sound of the man tracking that summer deer faded above the tree line, that Sabby Malloy would never come home again.

*

Old Man Malloy lay asleep on the sofa, his legs dangling over the side. Empty plates and cups cluttered the living room table. Drawn curtains kept out the light. Chaz straightened up the mess, cleared dishes into the sink, and threw out the garbage. He took a seat on the coffee table and gently prodded his father.

'Da, wake up, it's time tae go tae work.'

'Is that you, Sabby?' Old Man Malloy rubbed his eyes.

'No, it's jist me,' replied Chaz.

'Ur ye still wearen that dress?'

'It doesnae matter what I'm wearen.'

'Ur ye aff yer heid?'

'I'll never wear a dress again if that's what makes ye happy.'

Old Man Malloy sat up on the couch and reached for his tobacco. Chaz could see his hands shake as he fumbled for a cigarette paper. He gave up and handed the tin to Chaz. 'Could ye make wan fur me? I cannae see a thing.'

Chaz was used to rolling cigarettes for his mother but his father Old Man Malloy had never asked he do the same for him.

'Roll wan fur yersel if ye want,' Old Man Malloy added.

'I don't smoke,' said Chaz, running his tongue along the gummed edge of paper.

'What dae ye say the morra mornen, soon as I get back from work, we take a walk up the doocot? Put out a coupla birds,' said Old Man Malloy.

'Can I bring ma magic wand?'

'Yer what?'

'Magic wand. I found it up the burn. It can make people disappear.'

'As long as ye don't put a spell oan me.'

'I might turn ye intae a deer,' said Chaz.

'It's a deal. Now go and make me a cuppa tea while I get ready fur work.'

Later that night Chaz entered his parents' bedroom and began to clear his mother's clothes from her wardrobe. He carefully folded them and stacked them by the door. When he'd finished he took off his mother's dress and placed it neatly on top of the pile. Different voices rose up from the street.

Young Chaz Malloy lay naked on top of his parents' bed and listened. Voices of children called out the names of other children. Kind voices. Cruel voices. Living, vital voices. Voices of the heart.

Ian Macpherson

SALMON CHAMAREEMO

A major coup for Florette's writing group. A.L. Kennedy has agreed to come and read. Prestigious venue. Great interest. This, apparently, is fan*tast*ic news. I'm delegated to collect the legendary author from the station. Trouble is, I haven't a clue what he looks like.

I was pondering this problem as the 18:41 from Glasgow Central pulled in. Perhaps I should phone Florette and admit this gap in my knowledge. Not possible, unfortunately. I'd waxed lyrical on the subject that very day. Superb talent. Huge fan. That sort of thing. Perhaps, I ventured, our greatest living writer. I felt safe in assuming he *was* a writer. The living bit too seemed a pretty good bet. But these were my only clues. And the train had just sighed to a halt.

The brain works fast in these situations. What does an author look like? I was no great expert on the subject, but it seemed likely, at the very least, that he'd be drunk. Hemingway. Behan. The little Welsh chap. It wasn't much to go on, but most of the passengers strode past me towards the exit. All I had to do was wait for the drunk who didn't.

The crowd dispersed. Odd. All that remained was a lone woman. Bit of a mature student look. She stood there, possibly waiting for her boyfriend, while I tut tutted, examined my watch, fingered the cavernous wastelands of my trouser pockets. The outward signs of exasperation. The woman looked agitated. Paced around for a while. Then she began rooting through her bag. A book cover surfaced in the jumble.

Now this was uncanny. The book was by none other than A.L. Kennedy himself. What a stroke of luck. I was about to ask if she had any idea what he looked like when the train doors were prised open from the inside and a large man staggered blinking into the sunlight. Hat askew. Shirt tails out. The contents of his briefcase tumbling earthward. And singing 'Salmon Chamareemo' at the top of his voice. Now that's what I call a writer.

I hurried over and helped him retrieve his notes. Let me rephrase that. I hurried over and retrieved his notes. *He* decided to relieve himself onto the track. He fumbled beneath the generous folds of his stomach, but was unable to locate his trousers. He then abandoned plan A and decided to light the tip end of a cigarette instead. This attention to the minutiae of the writer's persona marked him down as the genuine article. I'd obviously found my man.

I waved the collected papers under his nose and made for the exit. He followed me, like a very large two-year-old, out of the station. I'd been right about the drink, as I knew I would be. All I had to do now was keep him away from prostitutes and brawls. At least until I'd got him to the venue.

The journey from station to venue was fraught with peril. I managed to pour him into the last remaining taxi but he positively cascaded out the other side. They'd left the child lock off. He tried several times to pay for the journey, by which time the woman had given up on her boyfriend and commandeered the taxi. I couldn't help feeling that a walk and a good cry might have suited her better in the circumstances. Added to which, she must have been aware of who Al was, and could so easily have shown deference to his genius. But such is the modern world.

So we walked. We visited several bars en route and here's a curious thing. The bar staff in all six obviously knew him but referred to him throughout as Frank. Wily ruse this. The alias. Anonymity. Very important for a writer.

I also humoured him on the brothel front. I had no choice in the matter, to be honest. He literally dragged me there. I must say, though, as brothels go it was very discreet. To the untrained eye a typical suburban semi. Well-trimmed hedge. Volvo. There were even a few kids dotted about to fool the authorities. The madam, a homely woman with a child under each arm, seemed consumed by rage as she hurled insult after insult at poor old Al, who was trying to urinate against the cotoneaster. Writers and prostitutes! An explosive mix.

I got the distinct impression, after the door had been slammed and double bolted, that Al was *persona non grata* in that particular establishment and that sexual gratification was out of the question. On that occasion at least.

The half-mile journey between brothel and arts centre passed without further incident, if we exclude a brief tango with a post box. He also attempted to serenade a woman whose name was *not* Delilah and woo a florist with her own flowers. Invoice to follow.

Some time later we negotiated the automatic doors of the venue. After a fashion. As I staggered through the foyer with Al declaring his undying love and promising 'to take me away from all this', I noticed that Florette was deep in conversation with a woman. Bit of a mature student look. She seemed vaguely familiar, but I was too busy trying to get Al's orchids out of my face to give it much thought.

I finally managed to prop him up at the bar, and left him there, happily slurring at the bar staff and trying to stuff his mangled bouquet in someone else's pint. And get this. As I was leaving, a barman said, 'Still at the bank, Frank?' Good old Al. What a guy. Not only the false name, but a false profession to boot. He was well covered on the privacy front.

The foyer, by the time I got back to it, was empty. The audience had taken their seats. But what about the star attraction? I noticed a table of his books taking pride of place in the centre of the room. Tons of the things. I wondered where he found time to write 'em, to be honest. But there, at any rate, they were.

I brushed past them into the auditorium. The lights were down on the audience. I peered into the darkness but couldn't see a thing.

'Florette,' I hissed. 'Are you in there?'

'I'm in the middle of a haiku,' she replied. 'And I'm over here.' I finally made her out, fully spotlit, behind the microphone.

'So you are,' I said. 'Do go on.'

She began to explain, to murmurs of approval from the audience, that it was very difficult to read a haiku in two parts. Why? I didn't catch that bit. I'd just noticed something which chilled the hairs on the back of my neck. Pacing in the shadows offstage, rigid with concentration, was the vaguely familiar woman.

What on earth was she up to? She must have followed us here. Granted, she got here first, but this was probably just a subtle way of covering her tracks. She had then inveigled herself into Florette's confidence. And now here she was. Looking for her footnote in history. There was no way the great man was going on that stage. I could see the headlines now.

'Kennedy Shooting: Woman Held.'

I rushed out of the auditorium without a single thought for my own personal safety.

Into the bar. No Al.

'Where's Al?'

'Who's Al?'

I said nothing. *I* wasn't going to blow his cover.

I rushed back out. Where could he possibly be? The gents. Of course. I rushed in. Two Jeremys. One Murdoch. And a man who refused to give his name without a warrant.

I rushed out. Pandemonium. What sounded like a prison riot. Coming straight from the ladies. I had obviously found my man. Again. And then I remembered the not-so-small matter of the stalker. First things first. I rushed over to the box office.

'I think you'd better call the police,' I panted.

'We already have.'

'Excellent work. You spotted her too.'

I rushed back into the auditorium.

But what's this?

The would-be assassin was standing onstage. Reading from one of Al's books if you please. And the audience? The audience was rapt. *Rapt!* Mass hypnosis? I'm no expert, but I knew one thing: I had to get Al out of here. It was nothing less than a madhouse.

When I returned to the foyer a troupe of women was filing out of the ladies. Cackling.

Bad sign.

I waited till the cackling had died off in the distance and made my way, very tentatively, inside. I knew the risks, but I needn't have worried. In the middle of the floor of the ladies, everything askew and smiling beatifically, sat Scotland's greatest living author.

I was in the act of hoicking him onto a lavatory seat when a police officer came in. Followed by – difficult to believe but it was that sort of evening – the madam. No kids. And she was speechless with rage.

The officer spoke for both of them.

'Come along then, Frank,' he said. 'Time for beddy-byes.'

So that was it. The poor woman was being forced to accept an unwanted client by a bent cop. My attempt to remonstrate on her behalf was met by a slap across the face. Which I accepted with good grace. And as Al staggered out of the ladies with his pathetic entourage I looked on with a strange mix of admiration and yet, somehow, moral revulsion.

Drink. Prostitutes. Brawls. I found myself wondering if writers indulge in this sort of carry-on for pleasure or research when I was interrupted in my reverie by the excited babble of female voices. 'Scotland's greatest living etc.' That sort of thing. They'd obviously met Al in the foyer. They seemed less thrilled to see *me* – loitering with intent, they called it – so I indulged in a symbolic hand wash, mumbled something about the Kennedy shooting, and left.

The foyer was packed. An enormous queue wound in ever increasing circles up to the table. And our stalker? Holding court at the self-same table. Twirling a biro as if she owned the thing. Gaily defacing copies of Al's life's work.

I was mulling this over in bed that night when Florette said something which stunned me to the very core of my beliefs.

'The less said about a certain matter the better,' she said, 'but I thought A.L. was fan*tas*tic tonight.'

I'm none the wiser to this day as to what the certain matter might have been, but no, I thought, Al was *not* fantastic. Al was an insult to a noble calling. Florette, it seems, had bought straight into the notion of the great writer as male, boorish and drunk. Time, perhaps, to consign that hoary old cliché to the reference library of history.

I said nothing – the situation with Florette seemed a trifle delicate at that point – but I did entertain a rather odd thought. In a funny sort of way the stalker – deranged, no doubt, but not obviously armed, unless we include the casually twirled pen – had probably saved the night.

Better all round, perhaps, if the great man himself had been a woman.

Andy Manders

NIGHT NIGHT

So really, my dear, the moral of the story ... the moral ... of the story ... the *moral* of the story ... is – doesni matter if it's death or dying, the fiery claw or the Cake Monster King, poverty, recession, the cops or jist the usual dark creeping in – the scareder you are, the braver you're gonni have ti be in the end. That's the moral, that's the story. Jist how it is, I'm afraid: the way o'it. The braver you'll be in the end. Gonni let me pit the light oot now, darling? Get a beer. Be a Big Girl and that. You that is. Go ti sleep now, darling?

I was telling wee Katie her story, same as always, earache or no. It crossed my mind I wasni helping, though she'd been totally definitely asleep for quite a while now. Bent owre her double I was, stroking the cold sweated band of her hair, I was telling her her story. Same as always. Though I was scared too I wasni gonni show her that, even if she was asleep. Wee Katie was like that: doesni matter if they're asleep or no, what bairns tak in. So I'm telling her her story.

A long, long time ago in Dwamland. We hadni been there a while. Doon the tracts of our past. When I put her in she jist huggles tighter ti my old blanket and howls. An hour ago it must be. She howls and I wish ti God I could stop her. In the end I tell her about how when I was wee and had toothache Bathgate Granny stuck whisky in ma ear. *You said it was toothache*, she sobs and her wee face fights ti smile. *Jist talk for a while. I like listening*, she says.

Aye well, you didni know your great-granny. She was from Skye and had to walk three miles to school every morning and the same back when she was your age. So I tell her about her great-granny, wonderin why I havni before. The coming south, the going into service, the kirk, the pandrops and the Island friends, the Gaelic and how she hadni taught Nana a word – what does that say? – and the gairden and the jam and the jeely-bag drippin and the songs and the bag slung up at the back of the door for the butcher in the morning and the radio and folk roond and the house full at New Year wi music and the stories they telt.

She's gone off before I get ti the end, which is guid, sure, but even if we never used to manage it aw that often, I used to like ti talk about it after, check out what she thinks. She says I go on a bit; likes the stories jist.

It must have started aftir we shifted her from oor bed ti her ain. Missing her mum. She couldni get ti sleep. Book after book we'd do, telling after telling, before giving up and just shifting her through later, praying she'd no wake from the clattering. Aw winter the pair of us walking about like we'd just shattirt aw the lightbulbs, while the health visitor's suggesting we steel our hearts and let her scream. Aye go on then. We managed seven minutes and didn't speak for a week for the guilt.

The books keep her awake, she says. Stimulate her mind. Wee Katie, sat there swinging her legs on the surgery chair, nods, understood at last.

A story by mouth, she says. The health visitor nods. We're just in the way really, her mither and me. Let the professionals handle it.

She can see the pictures inside her heid, they agree. Listen ti the words and the sounds of them. Doesni matter what it is apparently, first thing that comes ti ye, whatever. Make it up. At first it was jist rubbish, something ti take the silence away, onything really. Then aftir a while they start ti tak shape, something ti fill the silence wi. The same folk crop up again and again and I can see them for who they are.

Dwamland. Every so often I usedti stop a bit and think *where the fuck did that come frae then eh?* Katie lookin at me, checkin I'm awake. Usually we'd still do a book or two first, get her relaxed, then it was Dwamland. Unstimulate her mind.

It went on a lot for a long time. I loved it. After the first week I was creepin oot o bed to write them down for a while before I noticed that was changin it. I don't remember when it stopped or how, if it petered away gradually or just one night and then another wi'oot. Either way I do mind thinkin the sore-oppressed, previously chipper Dwamlander populace might be a tad miffed to be left there, hangin aw ponderous owre their destiny like that. Worse if they could see it happenin, our slow disillusionment with their previously endearing, weirdly purposeful little lives. Mibbe that'd be what'd finally bring down that bastard cake-scoffing King.

Only it hasni stopped, has it? It wasni an end. Not now. *Would you like a story?* Can you turn the music down, she says, it's hurtin my ear. *Then a story?* Then a story. I canni hear a thing, but still I make a pantomime trampin oot the door, down ti pit the music – that isni on – off.

And once she's off too I jist must have kept goin. The Dwamland folk hadni got rid of their King ataw and their lives went on in jist the same odd morally illustrative and instructive fashion: bein wise, pursuin justice, findin love and losin it, gettin over it, on wi it, thru it, past it, tellin stories thereafter, sharing a laugh. Next thing I know is the tears rollin down my cheeks and I'm wandrin off on the time me and her mither – who should be home by now – went up tae Kildrummy for the International Soup Festival and got attacked by rooks hitchin the back-road out of Leochel Cushnie. Ye couldni mak it up. We'd to fend them off with sticks. It was hellish. Worse than you'd think. I was telling her how you hear aw they stories about folk gettin savaged by bonxies and how it was worse than that. I was wonderin if perhaps I'd over-stressed the sheer black fury o it aw, what wi that and the bit about how we'd tae crawl like soldiers along a ditch, how it was that that was what led to the point of her maist likely conception, when I thought I heard a knock at the door.

Shit.

Wee Katie was like that, it doesni matter if they're asleep or no, what bairns tak in.

Theresa Muñoz

FIGHT

judging from the sounds
in the kitchen
you're building a sandwich
and thinking
what a mess we're making,
living together

in another room
I'm buried under the covers
listening to the radio
talk nonsense
and conjuring you
when you were younger:

on your family's porch steps
with your brothers –
hair side-shed, short trousers
your eyes soft
in that picture

how things could be
if we didn't know
each other

never my breathing
rippling
the blankets

and you
getting up, walking
opening the cupboards

John Murray

TWELVE RUNES

Ash
Black buds slow to leaf,
slow to fall
Hammer wood, hard as frost

Aspen
Music in the wind top
Martyrs pinned to your wood
Suckers below ground

Beech
Vaulted canopy rising
From muscular gothic,
Sandals through brown leaves

Birch
Supple twigs in a soft breeze
Bundled to chastise,
White paper bark peels

Box
Chessmen move
Confined to the board
Parterre to bigger visions

Elder
Hollow stemmed
Musky and purple mouthed
Pea-shooter or flute?

Haw
Drops of blood in the hedge
Scent of the cowshed
The old homestead

Oak
Maker of galls,
of joists and masts
Ant armies on the move

Rowan
Bumpers of spring wine
Bitter jelly for deer meat,
Ghosts at bay

Sloe
White flower on thorn-wood
Makes the walking stick,
Bears black and bitter fruit

Willow
Wood too wet to burn
Weaves baskets
Sends balls over boundaries

Yew
Pinned to the grave
Arrows across millennia,
Green in your own season

Ronnie Nixon

ART PRIZE

'Ma?' I shout. 'Ma!'

'Whit?'

'I cannae find ma school troosers.'

'They're in the bin, son,' she shouts back. 'I couldnae sort them and I'm no buying you another pair.'

I rummage aboot, find ma black jeans, get dressed and go through the kitchen.

'They troosers had hash holes aw doon the crotch and leg,' she says banging a plate of toast doon on the table. She takes a long drag on her fag, tilts her heid back, hauf shuts her eyes and blows smoke all ower the toast. She gies me a long look. 'Since when did you bother about whit you wear tae the school?'

I sit doon, cross ma eyes and stick oot ma tongue.

She leans ower and skelps the back of ma heid. 'You'll stay like that, ya cheeky wee fucker.'

I poke aboot the plate, find the least burnt bit, and marmalade it.

'And another thing,' she says staring intae her compact like she's aboot tae gie hersel a big kiss, 'it's no like you to get oot your bed withoot me shouting at you till I'm part demented. Think I was born yesterday? Eh? You'd better be going intae that school, Danny! I'm sick tae death getting hassled aboot you dogging it. Got enough on my plate withoot that bloody nonsense.'

'I'm going.'

'Better be.'

'This toast's boggin.'

'Gie me five minutes, son.' She smears on mair lipstick. 'I'll get you oot, I'm needing smokes.'

I look at the kitchen clock.

'Cannae wait, Ma.' I shove the rest of the toast intae ma mooth and beat it doon the hall.

She yells after me, 'Danny Kelso, what the hell are you up tae? You'd better no be dogging it again. I'm warning you!'

I grab ma jacket and shoot oot the front door.

*

Oor whole class is getting going. Even though it's just me, Angela McGilvary and Stephen Wilks that got oor designs picked. There's a bus coming tae take us tae the toon hall. Miss Doyle telt us the heid of the education department and the heid of the stationery company are gonnae be there. The company's heid's picking the best wan tae put on the front cover of their new stationery catalogue. The winner's getting a brand new computer and the art department's getting wan tae.

I get tae the school bang on nine, juke through the gap in the fence, and cut across the car park.

'Ho! Kelso!' Molloy, wan of the fifth years, shouts. 'Yer da's a fucking jailbirdjunkie and yer maw's a fucking hoor!'

He's wi three of his team. They're huddled behind the boiler hoose, sharing a fag.

I gie them the finger and run like fuck.

Mr McGrain, ma reggy teacher, comes ower and rubs his eyes when he sees me sitting there.

He turns tae the class. 'Can any of yous tell me who this pupil is? I don't think I've seen him before.'

The class burst oot laughing.

Sharon Beattie gets up, makes a big deal of staring ower at me and says, 'I've never seen him afore either, sir. Mibby he's an urban terrorist, sir. Infiltratin oor ranks, sir!'

They all burst oot laughing again.

I feel a beamer coming on.

McGrain smiles at the class like they're all big pals of his. 'And what, may I ask, do we owe this rare visit to, Mister Kelso?'

I cross ma arms and stare doon at my trainers.

Willie Devany shouts oot, 'He thinks he's gonnae win the computer, sir!'

I feel ma beamer getting hotter.

I just manage tae stop masel fae shouting at Devany tae fuck right off. Cunt's deid at hauf-three. Then I think, how am I gonnae gie him a doing if I'm carrying a computer hame?

*

Miss Doyle's no got a class first period so we all go up tae her room after reggy. I sit up the back. Mr Cunningham, the heid of the art department, is there. He starts giein us a talk about how we're representing the school and anyone oot of order will be sorry aboot it for the rest of the year.

He says it three times.

'And who, Miss Doyle,' Cunningham says pulling at his daft wee goatee beard, 'are the ones whose designs have been chosen?'

'Stephen Wilks, Angela McGilvary, and Danny Kelso,' Miss Doyle says.

She looks ower and gies me a big smile.

I gie her a wee wave.

Cunningham glares at me then turns and gies Miss Doyle a look to let her know he thinks she's off her fucking trolley.

'Daniel Kelso,' he says. 'I hope your behaviour has improved since you were in my class last year. I'm not sure if it was up to me that I'd let a boy like you go on this outing.' He cranes his scraggy neck oot, and peers at me wi his wee marbly eyes – his coupon lights up like he's just found oot he's copped the winning lotto numbers.

'You're not wearing a tie, Kelso! School uniform, Kelso! You can't represent the school if you're not in school uniform.'

The cunt smirks, shakes his heid at Miss Doyle, and gies her a *there-you-go* look.

Miss Doyle's in her desk like a shot. She pulls oot a school tie, walks up the back of the class, and hands me it. 'Put that on, Danny.'

Cunningham gies me a dirty look. You can tell he's no exactly happy wi Miss Doyle either.

'Just remember 3C' – he fucking says it again – 'you're representing the school and anyone' – he stares right at me – '*anyone,* out of order, is for the high jump! If I hear of – '

Thank Christ.

The janny sticks his heid round the door and says, 'That's the coach here, Miss Doyle.'

We all line up and go doon the car park.

Hughes, the Deputy Heid, is standing talking tae the driver.

Miss Doyle telt us he's coming because the education heid's gonnae be there. He goes ower tae Miss Doyle. The two of them walk off a bit. I can just hear Hughes saying ma name, but I cannae make oot anything else.

Sharon Beattie says tae me ma design's brilliant, it's definitely gonnae win. We start talking aboot whether they'll have sausage rolls at the buffet.

Hughes glowers ower at us.

'Quiet there!' he yells. 'Line up properly, 3C!'

He walks up and doon us wi his hands behind his back, like he's the Duke of Edinburgh inspecting the fucking troops. When he's done he goes ower and says something tae Miss Doyle. They look like they're arguing.

He turns round and walks towards us.

Miss Doyle has shut her eyes.

He stops haufway, and points tae the ground.

'Kelso! Here!' he shouts.

You'd think he was calling a fucking dug.

'Did you hear me, Kelso?'

I stare at the cunt.

'Come over here this instant!' he screams.

I slowly step oot the line, walk ower.

He points at my legs.

'What are they, Kelso?'

'Legs,' I says.

His coupon goes pure beetroot. He leans forward and screeches right intae my face, 'Don't be insolent, boy!' Spit's flying fucking everywhere.

I wipe ma sleeve across ma face.

He wheeks round tae Miss Doyle. 'Miss Doyle,' he says. 'This boy is not coming. Those are denims he's wearing.'

I look at her.

She's staring at her shoes and shaking her heid.

'You stay there, Kelso,' he says. 'The rest of you get in the coach.'

There's total silence.

The class doesnae move.

'In the coach! NOW!' he screams.

They keep staring at him.

Miss Doyle says, 'Come on, 3C. Into the coach.'

They start moving. Angela McGilvary's greetin.

Hughes cannae look me in the eye. He stares up at the sky and says, 'And you. Kelso. Report to the office. Tell Mrs Coghill that Mr Hughes says you're in detention until your class gets back.'

'Fuck off, Hughes,' I say, and walk oot the school.

*

I found oot a couple of days later that a lassie fae another school won the computer.

I cannae help thinking. If Miss Doyle had had a spare pair of troosers in her desk – I'd have fuckin won it.

Jane Rawlinson

STONE FURNITURE
Skara Brae, Orkney, 3500BC

On the day that I was born
My mother found for me
To save for my stone dresser
A grey pebble polished by the sea.

The day I was betrothed
My true love gave to me
A barred sea hawk's feather
To keep for my stone dresser
With my grey pebble polished by the sea.

The day that I was wed
My mother made for me
A clay cooking pot
To put on my stone dresser
With my barred sea hawk's feather
And my grey pebble polished by the sea.

The day our son was born
My husband carved for me
A yellow seal's tooth
To adorn my stone dresser
With my clay cooking pot
My barred sea hawk's feather
And my grey pebble polished by the sea.

The day my mother died
She bequeathed to me
Her woven willow basket
To display on my stone dresser
With my carved seal's tooth
Clay cooking pot
Barred sea hawk's feather
And my grey pebble polished by the sea.

The day the raiders came
And slew my family
They stole from my stone dresser
Most of my treasure
My carved seal's tooth,
Clay cooking pot
And the willow basket filled with barley.

But my barred sea hawk's feather
I bade the wind blow free
And my grey polished pebble
I slipped back into the sea.

Jane Rawlinson

THRESHING THE WIND

Windmills, thought Margo Thom. She stood at the farmhouse door and looked across the deep valley to the sweeping, gorse-topped hill beyond. There, in her mind's eye, great steel giants spun their arms across the sky. She could already feel the hum of the turbines, as if the electricity they generated turned on a warm, bright bulb inside her. The sort that her husband might hang in the barn over a litter of puppies when the cold outside was sharp enough to kill.

Strange, she thought, at her age, with the family grown up and gone that she felt this restlessness, this craving for something to happen. Margo was so often alone that the past had become more real to her than the present. Her life was peopled with ghosts. Her dead parents. Her brothers and sisters. Her own children, who were now scattered all over the globe. She tried to shoo them away, but they took no notice.

'You are not really here but I am,' she protested.

'Prove it,' they seemed to reply.

How could she when life carried on just as it would if she were dead and buried? Hens clucked in dust baths at her feet. Cattle swished their tails to fend off flies. Lapwings called, the shadow of a buzzard drifted over the sea of ripening barley. After all these years, she felt as if she might suffocate in the quiet sameness of the unfolding seasons.

At the turn of the year, it was the snow that hemmed her in. Throughout the winter, Margo kept the fire stacked with coal and logs, took food from the freezer, kneaded her own dough and waited until Iain had time enough to spare from feeding the beasts to take the tractor and carve a glistening blue-white tunnel the six miles to the main road. In summer, the weight of heat was equally oppressive. It pinned her to the valley floor like a butterfly in a display case. Of course they had a car, but Margo had never learnt to drive. There was never time. After lambing came calving, followed by silage, then harvest, before darkness and frost closed in again as tight as a vice.

But a wind farm meant a road. A real, solid, black road. She yearned for it to snake up the valley sloughing its tarmac skin. She imagined the contractors' vehicles grinding up the slope and the slow piecing together of the windmills. How they would strain against the leash until that magical moment when their arms were set free. After that would come maintenance workers. Tourists. They would bring wives and children. They would pass her door and perhaps stop to talk as she hung out the washing or tended her vegetables. She would offer them scones and tea and hear about their lives.

'Wind farm!' sneered Iain when the idea was first mooted. 'And pigs might fly.'

Margo wondered whether it was the word 'farm' that upset him. Perhaps the gentle, persistent motion of the arms seemed to him too easy, too far removed from the hard thrust of ploughshare into soil, the unrelenting toil of planting and nurturing, the sweat of the harvest, the lowing demands of beasts in the byre. To Iain, the wind was a dangerous foe which threatened his livelihood.

Onto the ground in front of the doorstep, Margo tipped a saucepan of scraps, the hard heel of bread, the potato peel, porridge scrapings, turnip trimmings, all boiled up together with bran into a pungent, glutinous mess. The chickens came running. Clucked their contentment as they ate. Perhaps she would put up a sign. Free Range Eggs for Sale. So much was possible she thought as she turned her back on the unpeopled valley and the searing yellow gorse-clad hill and went indoors to start the tea.

So much was possible. So many ideas came to her as she chopped onions and meat and browned them in the pan. By the time the potatoes had crumbled into a floury cream, Margo's farm shop was selling carrots and leeks, purple jars of bramble jelly, yard-long sticks of rhubarb. Her living room had become a tea room.

Then Iain came home. Without a word, he stepped out of his boots at the front door and washed his hands at the sink. Margo always had the tea ready at precisely the same time. Sometimes she chafed at the inflexibility of the routine, but today she welcomed it. There had been such an outcry over the wind farm that a Public Inquiry had been held. Today the Secretary of State would give his decision.

Margo and Iain ate in silence in front of the six o'clock news. There was no need to say anything. The food was the usual home-bred lamb stew, no surprises. Each knew exactly what the other had been doing all day. The news from the Middle East was too remote to cause comment. As for what preoccupied Margo, there was nothing she could say that would not cause contention, for she was as much in favour the wind farm project as Iain was against it.

When the plates were empty, Margo got up and took them into the kitchen. She returned promptly with two servings of pie made from the last of the meagre apple crop greased with custard, just as the local news came on. The Secretary of State had considered the objections against the projected wind farm and upheld them.

Iain ate his first mouthful of pie without comment. Margo, her appetite suddenly gone, put down her bowl, got up and went outside. She crossed the barren yard and kept on walking. Down the track and over the mud-clarted bridge. Up the meadow, weaving through the brown and white cattle, across the high field where lambs played king of the castle on the mound of a ruined dwelling.

She thought of the objectors in their big cars as she marched up the forest track. She thought of them on the patios of their distended cottages, sizzling barbecues on summer evenings. On she surged following deer tracks through the gorse, imagining their foreign holidays, private schools and central heating. On she went, emerging at last onto the open hill top, striding towards the summit.

Margo was wafer thin, tough and straight as a silver birch. As she crested the brow the wind slammed into her. She leant into it, feeling her heart quicken and her muscles tauten and hum like turbines throbbing into use. She glanced down at the toy farm below. The tiny fields. The ant-like cattle and pinprick sheep. The smallness of her life.

But up here, Margo was part of something greater. Here, beneath the great dome of sky with its sweeping white clouds the wind strengthened her. She turned her back on the croft and the valley. Instinctively, she faced into the current of air and felt her hair lift and stream out behind her. Then slowly, slowly her arms begin to rise and then to spin. She stood there defiantly, a giant, her arms moving in great circles against the sky as her body charged with energy and the words throbbed through her skull, 'I am. I am. I am.'

James Sinclair

ABANDONED ON STAC AN ARMIN

1. THE GREAT ADVENTURE

In the year of our Lord 1726, a first trip to Stac an Armin
with sunshine and laughter, as we all
gathered for communion on Village Bay's shingly beach.
Missionary blessing our venture with the Almighty.

Mother was fussing over buttons on my jacket,
her warm hands ruffling through my thick, black hair.
My little brothers tugged at ill-fitting breeches
laughing and poking fun at my first straggly beard.

Elizabeth Jane, silent, quietly slipped soft fingers
into mine, a sparkle dancing in her dark eyes
and with a final check of equipment, we were away.
A stout shove and this boat slipping into water.

Strong arms dragged hard on oar, pulling away,
taking us away from waving hand and final farewell.
My father sat calmly sucking upon his clay pipe.
His words from the day before ringing in my ears.

'Son, this is where you become a man.
The community is depending on you.
You have to be strong and hold your tongue.'

Oars slapped a faltering rhythm on the flat ocean,
a windless sea, sluggish, rolled on to the horizon
and a sound began to build inside my head,
the chatter and shrill notes of endless bickering.

A million gannets in a frenzy were tearing at the sky.
They flew in haphazard arcs, plummeting from on high,
raining down like arrows, piercing the side of the ocean
and there rising before us, a giant's fang, Stac an Armin.

2. ABANDONED

Three weeks we should have been here,
now days slip one carelessly into another.
A whole winter stuck upon this steep skerry,
abandoned with little hope of reprieve.
The dogs on Hirta have a better life than us.

We scurry and scavenge, dirty like rats
among these high crags, man gone feral.
My beard reaches down to my chest, my feet
have grown into claws, my fingers
like talons, they tear at raw rib-cages.

Three days now these gales have blown,
a chill wind carries shiploads of sleet and snow.
As we huddle together like puffins in our burrow
clinging to one another in the hope of warmth.
William John, he has been our rock of faith –

standing like a sentinel on the point
day after day, spyglass clamped to his one good eye.
Calmly scanning all the way out past Stac Lee
across the short distance between here and home.
At night he sings psalms and tells Bible stories.

Last night I dreamt that I was standing
on a narrow ledge, looking out towards Hirta,
my body felt empty and as light as a feather.
Launching myself over the edge, my arms
turned into broad wings as I found the power of flight.

There I was, soaring high into the sky,
circling my beloved isles, looking for my mother's house.
Down below I saw Elizabeth Jane, standing alone
on Village Street, and as I flew down to her
she opened her arms and smiled.

3. HOMECOMING

In the month of April 1727 we were met by the stare of
    strangers
whose shocked eyes took in our wild appearance.
The only familiar face, Charles Arnold sitting at the helm,
unsure why his old bones had lived on this long,
uncertain why it was his job to deliver this message.

And when the news came, we boys failed to understand
but our elders knew, my father slumping into a heap.
I watched the shine in William John's eyes ebb away
and George Andrew poured his sickness over the side.
All the while, steady oarsmen were pulling us home.

A terrible pain rose, squeezing my chest, until fit to burst
as my breathing laboured and a dryness filled my mouth.
Closer and closer we came and in one awful moment
I wished hard that they'd left us on that rock to die.
All too soon the keel scraped up over shingled stones.

On shore, a silent gathering of waiting children.
The steward, dark-suited, made to speak.
'Thank God you're all safe, the Lord has truly been merciful!'
William John fell down on his knees, letting out a scream.
'How much can one man bear, is it God's will to break us?'

Shaking himself to pieces, his sobbing such a pitiful sound.
Elizabeth Jane, alive, took me and my father by the hand,
saying 'Come home with me for I have no one left,'
and she led us with words of gentle encouragement
towards the empty houses, our feet encased in stone.

Nancy Somerville

BREAKING AWAY

In a living-room, a wooden crate
going nowhere but moving,
shifting and straining
to keep in what's pushing out:
a snow leopard.
Old wood groaning to rusty nails
twisting into its untouched heart,
orange stains on splintering fresh cream.

One clawing paw scrapes through,
red beadlets on grey wood
and soft fur.
The crate complains but holds
shakily, not fast,
it can't last.

Gerda Stevenson

LAST SUNDAY
For Simon MacKenzie

Your skin glares yellow as lemon peel,
hairless head a bloated mask.
Only a wrist band confirms you're here,
till lips part, and in quiet Gaelic tones
you thank me for coming, ask for news
of my family. It seems like a taunt
to say we're well, so I tell you instead
my son has your language, passed
the exam with flying colours.
Mouth and eyelids flicker approval
as you fumble at nostrils to adjust
the oxygen's angle, pin cushion hand
sprouting wires. You lower its palm
into mine. We hold silence.

The hospice doors wheeze to a close
behind me. A robin flits onto a litter bin.
Gulls wheel on spring gusts
to the clink of a bare flagpole.

Andrew Stott

SHOES

They're mostly black. Some of them shine. The ones people will pick up tomorrow, or the day after, but the rest are dull. With dust.

I put my hand to one and wipe it across. It comes up thick in my fingers and I roll it around and then let it drop. So many shoes. So many unclaimed pairs of shoes. What? Do they forget? How can you forget about a pair of shoes? And this isn't the lot of them either. There's more through the back.

I pick up one pair. A black pair. And I look at the ticket. Lazenby it says. Twenty-third of September oh seven. Almost a year ago. I'm supposed to do a clear-out once a month. I thought I did a clear-out once a month.

I keep them for six months. That's what the sign says. Really I keep them for a lot longer. There's a green pair here. A ladies' pair. They belonged to a young girl. Maybe she was bringing them in for her mum. They just needed a bit of restitching. The girl was worried, upset. Maybe it was her that broke them. She never came back. Perhaps it was easier if her mum just lost them.

And a red pair. Of slip-on jobs. A ladies' shoe. I put new heels on. Who did they belong to? I can't remember. All the faces. They just blur.

Mary wore black shoes. She wore all different kinds of shoes but her everyday-go-out-to-work-shoes were black, without much of a heel. When we went out she used to wear things that stepped her up higher than me. And I used to say to her. I'd say, 'Don't do that, Mary. It makes me look short.' And she'd just laugh, and she'd say we were the same height. But we weren't. We weren't the same height at all.

What about this brown pair? I take them out and brush the dust off, and then get the dust out of the creases, and there's even dust inside. I claw it out and drop it. It floats to the floor. Now, what does the ticket say? Lazenby. Lazenby again? But there's no date. I turn it over. There's nothing on the back. The paper clip's started to rust on this one. Lazenby. There can't be that many Lazenbys.

I sit down on my stool and kick off the wall and I whizz down the way, and I spin as I go, and I end up in front of the tools. I overcooked that one. I use the bench to turn me round and I reach under the key machine and feel around and pull out some magazines and I drop them on the floor and I feel around again and pull out a telephone book. I wipe the dust off the edges and I open it and I flick through and I go to 'L'. Laing. Laurie. Lawrence. Lazenby. There are only two. Only two Lazenbys. I get up off the stool and walk through to the back of the shop. I pick up the phone. It's black with shoe polish, off my hands, off Mark's hands. Mary kept saying that I ought to get a new one. Why? It'll just get covered in polish. Maybe I should buff it up with the machine. Make it shine. I dial the number. You can hardly see the numbers, for the polish, and the years. There's no number nine left. When the hairdresser used to be upstairs I had to dial nine for an outside line. Not any more. They've left now. They left a long time ago. And now my door's locked.

The phone rings. Meep meep. Meep meep. Meep meep. It keeps ringing. I look across, into the front of the shop, and out of the window. It's difficult to see properly. There's crappy marks all over the window, left over from posters that people wanted me to let them put up and why should I stop them? As long as it's nothing bad.

Meep meep.

'The person you are calling is not available. Please try again later.'

Click.

That voice.

It's like Mary's.

I press the hangup key and then press to call again.

Meep meep meep meep meep meep meep meep mee…

Fuck.

I hold the phone in my hands and smear my thumb over the numbers. I bite my tongue. I press to call again.

Meep meep.

'The person you are calling is not available. Please try again later.'

A computer.

A computer that sounds like her.

There's a double beep.

I press the hangup key.

I wipe my face.

I key in the next number. Six six two. Three four five six.

Meep meep.

Meep meep.

Meep meep.

Meep meep.

Meep meep.

Meep meep.

'The person you are calling is unavailable. Please leave a message after the tone.'

Meeeeeeep.

'This is Roy's, the cobblers here, I'm calling about a pair you've left. Maybe two pairs actually. A brown pair and a black pair. Emm. You don't want to leave them more than six months because they take up space so I have to be rid of them because I've not got a lot of space. So if you could come and collect them, because otherwise they will have to go. So. Bye.'

He holds the phone in his hand. It's an age to him but moments to us. There are no thoughts but it builds in him. It's winding up, churning round and round inside him and he senses it coming and tries to hold it back but you can't hold back something like this and he brings the phone down with a crash onto the table and he expects it to break but it doesn't, it slips instead, perhaps with the years of shoe polish and it pings from his hand and the table and flies in an arc, a beautiful arc of white against the splattered black background of a million shoes in their holes in the wall, and it disappears, straight into one, into a shoe, with an empty thunk.

He holds his hand.

He's broken his hand, against the table.

Roy needs his hands.

He needs them to hold shoes. And keys.

But not today.

Today the door is locked.

So no customers can come in.

Roy was dreaming last night. He was dreaming about Egyptians, of Pharaohs, of Antony and Cleopatra, and Mary, when she was young, and she had dark hair all thick and everywhere and around her face and around his face but it got cold and he hugged Mary more and it felt colder so he squeezed her tighter and pressed his knees into the insides of hers but she felt colder again and he kissed her back, where his face was pressed, but still the chill was there and in him and around them and Mary kissed him, in the dream, but the kiss was cold and he opened his eyes. He turned away from Mary and pulled the duvet in around him and even pressed it down between them because, for a moment, his bottom had touched hers and she was so cold, and he had to get a good night's sleep because it was work tomorrow.

He slept in fits and starts.

When he got up, before the alarm went off, he knew something was wrong and he touched Mary and he shook her and he pulled her so she rolled over toward him and she didn't open her eyes.

He phoned for an ambulance. It came and then it left. Because there was nothing it could do.

He waited for the funeral director to arrive.

And they took Mary away.

And then Roy went to work. But he locked the door. And he stared at all the shoes.

Alison Swinfen

THE NEWS

Mrs Anderson?

Yes.

The tests show that the lump is cancerous.
There are two operations we can do.
We can take the lump away or we can take the whole
    breast

away.

I can do you the operation on Monday.

Yes.

We can take the lump or we can take the whole breast

away.

The whole breast and the lymph glands.

Your son?

Yes.

He'll be down here on Sunday?

Yes.

so you can stay with him on Sunday?

Yes.

Now have you thought about your operation?
Have you thought what you'd definitely prefer?

Yes.

So you'd definitely prefer that we take the whole breast

away.

Your son,

Yes.

the whole breast. You'd prefer we took the whole breast

away.

The one that suckled him
and nourished him.

that one,

we will take the whole one
the whole breast
away.

Away.

Away where?

Where do whole breasts go?

And the milk of
old that
filled Sunday's
son?

That is what you'd prefer?
That we take

we take

that we take the whole breast
whole,

that we take it

away.

Daryl Tayar

BACK COURT BODY

Sunset swallowed the red sandstone walls,
thunder tore the violet tissue of the sky.
Wildly he swung his spade in the back court,
ripped earth's mossy coat and flung it back.

The chill rain in his eyes didn't stop him,
nor the saddled-up dark rushing at him –
the shovel's gleam in windowlight kept him going,
digging the clay for a heap of bones.

Wet shirt sticking, boots puddling, fingers blue,
he dug up muck, bits of tarmac, broken knives,
a deposit of cinders – old firelight scattered –
even a rusty key to some long gone future.

Midnight. A toll of sore breath rang out;
the back court, uneasy, turned in her sleep.
He leaned on his spade. The hole was wide and deep,
a scratch on the heavy, dark face of the earth.

By dawn he had found a bed of wet rock
and two old pence he gave to his mother
to place on his eyes: a last goodbye. Then
he lay down in the mud and sang to the sky.

Jim Taylor

THE MUPPET SHOW ON ICE

At 7:58 I clocked in and followed the sound of slamming lockers. No cheeky banter in this dressing room. No fish factory Ally McCoists. No eye contact, even. Just get the overalls on, white hat, white wellies and go. Everyone in white except the foreman, shouting at people in his black coat and hat. 'You! New guy!' He pointed me to a spot near the start of the line. A girl stood next to me with a spoon on a suction hose and told me to watch. The machine about to spout fish was controlled by the scariest-looking guy I had ever seen. His name, marker-penned across the front of his bib, was Norman. I realised he hadn't written it there so's new folk would know what to call him. It was so no other person would touch his XXL oilskins. And I didn't want to look too closely, but I could swear Norman had the faces of two different people joined down the middle. He was looking over, but I wasn't keen to look back in case I ended up staring at him, and you didn't want to be staring at a guy like Norman.

Everyone looked up towards the top deck, where people were standing round a vat, elbows thrusting. 'The killers,' said the girl. Her name was Michelle, good looking in a tough way, blonde, about my age. 'It's going to be hard the day,' she warned. 'Lot of people didn't make it in.'

Then it started, the conveyor belt, empty at first, the noise rising to an almighty screech and suddenly the gutted salmon were through the machine and on us. Michelle scooped out the remaining slime as the fish sped past us towards a row of women who hosed and graded them. After a minute she handed me the spoon and stood back, watched for a second, gave me a thumbs up and walked away. I was ready to fly solo, but it wasn't long before my first crash. A second too long with some sticky bubble gum guts and before I knew it there was a pile-up, salmon cascading everywhere. I reached to pick one off the floor but there was a shout above the machines. Michelle was waving 'No' and jabbing her finger at the oncoming fish. All the while, as salmon spewed from his machine, Norman watched me with his unreadable expression. Then everything stopped and people looked up and down the line. There was a problem and for one horrible second I thought it was me, until I heard the foreman laying into someone in the distance. Then he walked past our section and saw the mess. 'Can someone make sure this muppet knows what he's doing?'

A wee guy I recognised from up the road was shoving a tower of polystyrene boxes along the floor. He seemed to be enjoying my predicament. With his two black eyes, ginger hair and evil smirk, he looked like The Joker. Michelle came to my side, grabbed a spoon and helped me sort out the fish that had spilled. One of the graders, Pearl, about forty with a sunbed tan and a hoarse laugh, gave me a dirty wink. 'Michelle'll keep you right.' Norman stepped forward and I tensed, uncertain if he was about to offer assistance or gut me like a wayward salmon, but then the machine fired up and he was back at his post.

My arm jerked and the spoon gurgled and swallowed until ten o'clock: breakfast time. The process workers shuffled out and the cleaners came in, hosing the swill down a sluice and outside, where angry gulls were wheeling and squawking. The cafeteria wasn't much friendlier a feeding ground. Everyone held their tray like a buffer, shielding their personal space, aware of the others without ever looking. It might be a mistake to sit in somebody's usual place, I thought, especially Norman's, as he took his fry-up to a corner between the door and the windows. Small groups gathered together, a crowd of women including Michelle and Pearl, a few Asian ladies, some older men. I made for the last vacant table, but before I could sit down a young squad appeared from behind me and grabbed all the chairs. 'Give it a bye, Muppet,' said The Joker, to the amusement of his pals.

I found a place next to the battered Christmas tree. Beside me the Asian women were speaking in their own language, but one broke off to ask me, 'You go to party?'

'Don't know. Where?'

'Tonight. North Star. Everybody go. You nice boy. Meet lady.'

They all giggled. I looked round the room and wondered if I wanted to socialise with my new workmates. The Joker seemed to have his eye on me while speaking in a low voice to his posse. They were the young team from up our way and for all I knew they were plotting to kill me. I say from up 'our way', but none of us were from up anywhere, really. We just all happened to live in that northerly estate where waifs and strays are housed. Norman sat alone, a Frosty the Snowman decoration on the wall above his massive head. He looked like Frankenstein dreaming of a white Christmas. The girls laughed at something Pearl said and they all glanced over at me.

'Maybe,' I said to the ladies. There was a late north bus some nights, commonly known as the Midnight Express, on account of its hour and the number of convicted drug dealers on board.

Chairs started scraping and there was a surge to the door as everyone went for a smoke. The sun was now slanting in over the snowy hills, bringing a fresh gleam to the tree's tired tinsel. I went to the windows and looked down at the jetty and loading bays. People were lighting their fags and starting to chat. Two seals sped through the sparkling water and I realised they were racing.

'Funnin,' said a deep voice. Norman was sitting at the other end of the windows, slowly wiping the yolk off his plate with a roll. He was definitely talking to me, but it was still hard to look into his amalgamated face.

'Eh … eh? Aye, the seals. Aye,' I nodded.

'You going back down there?' he asked me. This time I could detect irony and braced myself for some kind of put-down.

'Is that the break over? Sure, yeah.'

'You'd be surprised how many people don't make it past the first break,' he said.

'Really?' I asked, still unsure if he was giving me encouragement or a warning. 'I can see why,' I said. 'Lot of shouting and bawling.'

'Just don't let it bother you,' he replied, gradually standing up and continuing past me until he came to his full height. That was all very well for him to say, I thought. Who the hell was ever going to call Norman a muppet? He took his tray to the counter and walked out.

Down below, people were making their way inside. Michelle looked up and smiled. Watching from the back of the crowd was the young team. The Joker leered at me, shuffled his fist and mouthed 'wanker'.

Before the line started I mentioned the North Star to Michelle. Yes, of course she was going. Everyone was meeting in the Lounge first. I resented having to leave her when they ordered me to another part of the shed, to a machine that launched fish of various sizes out of different holes. Me and a Polish guy had to wait for boxes filling and replace them before they overflowed. When Jarek went for more empties, the foreman shouted from the other side of the shed to close number two. He stared at me and cupped his hands round his mouth. 'Close number two!' he repeated. As I looked round helplessly, Jarek reappeared and flipped a lever. 'How many times have I got to say it?' yelled the foreman as he stormed off.

I blew my cheeks out. 'That guy shouts a lot,' I said.

'If you working here you have to take shit,' Jarek told me dismissively.

My next job was shovelling ice into boxes of fish from a huge bin. When the bin was empty you shoved it away and dragged in a refill. The first time I tried this manoeuvre, I skidded and went on my dish, right in the path of a forklift, which had to brake hard not to impale me. The driver had a Jarl's Squad beard and a personalised number plate: 'Duff 1'. He watched me stand up and wipe blood from a grazed cheek. 'Slippy,' he commented, before shooting off.

In the end I was put with The Joker and his squad, stacking boxes onto palettes. Everyone was smaller than me, but they could all hurl their boxes onto the very top, whereas I had to wrestle mine up. No one said anything, but they didn't have to. I had already been established as The Muppet. The truck drivers and forklift guys had been giving the young ones plenty of stick, shouting at us to hurry up and get the last boxes stacked. Then the foreman came over and said, 'What's holding things up?' at which point The Joker launched into the most incredible tirade, a complete list of every curse and insult in the English language. He was screaming it all into the foreman's face, until the last and most shocking syllable of all, with which he redirected his mad eyes towards a grinning forklift man. Then, to the cheers of the drivers, he jerked his thumb towards them and told the foreman, 'Sort these tossers out, man.'

Unsure what to make of it, the foreman said to no one in particular, 'Let's get the job done,' and walked away. I was thinking The Joker might have his good points. At least he wasn't advising everyone just to take the crap and get on with it.

When a shout went up that the fish were finished and the day's work over, I hung back, let everyone move through the locker room and out to the car park. Some had cars, some shared taxis. I walked into town, to the library, which was open late, and inspected my sore face in the toilet. Just a scratch, not too bad, maybe even a good thing, seeing as every other guy in the place had an obvious chib mark or disfigurement. Upstairs in the reference section, I dozed in a soft seat with a magazine, turning a page whenever a noise woke me. Two hours later, as they started to shut shop, I sat up and noticed my right hand had closed into a permanent spoon-holding claw. It was sore to open it, but I reckoned I would still be able to handle a pint glass.

The Lounge was already heaving and I heard Pearl's laugh before I saw her. She was ordering a round of cocktails with rude names. 'Have you got everything you need for tonight?' she asked me. 'I've got E's, sulph ...'

'I'm okay the now thanks.'

'Well if you change your mind.' She was wearing a tight, low-cut T-shirt that showed her huge cleavage, pierced beer belly and tattooed bingo wings. Across her bust was a slogan: '100% fake'. She noticed me looking and squished herself into a mountain of tanned bosom. 'That's right, it's all bought and paid for!' Then she punched me gently on the arm. 'Come on, what are you having then?' She got me to relay drinks to the girls, standing in a crowd in the middle of the room.

Michelle thanked me for her Screaming Orgasm. 'I saw Pearl giving you a good show over there,' she said.

'The words "mutton" and "lamb" spring to mind.'

'Uch, Pearl's sound. She thinks you look like Matt Damon.'

'What do you think?'

She raised an eyebrow. 'A wee bit. What about me, who do I look like?' She put a fingertip to her chin and turned her profile.

'Duffy.'

'The singer?'

'No, the forklift truck driver.'

'Ha ha. That Duffy's got a bigger beard than me.'

'I'll take your word for it.'

I got drunk fast and before I knew it we were in the queue for the North Star. The sniffer dog went straight past Pearl. 'She's got a special way of hiding the stuff,' explained Michelle. The music was hardcore, a few people up, but most standing round like zombies. 'Welcome to the Death Star,' Michelle bellowed in my ear. I had only met these people the same day, but recognising them without their white hats on made it feel like a reunion of old comrades. Pearl was leaning over the bar getting another round in and the young barman looked scared. She was only one of a whole crowd of menacing drunks in front of him. The Joker was there, shoving in front of some of the drivers. He was looking for hassle, but there were no takers.

I sat down with Michelle and her pals, the only guy with eight girls. Norman was on the far side of the hall with his back to a pillar, staring through the mist like an Easter Island statue. 'What's the score with Norman's face?' I asked.

'A car accident,' explained Michelle. 'They had to rebuild him.'

All of a sudden, a plastic tumbler skited off the top of my head. When I turned round no one was looking my way, but The Joker's gang were within range. 'Guess they don't like strangers muscling in on their women round these parts.'

'Just ignore it. Come on,' she said, leading me onto the floor. The whole time we were up, The Joker was giving me the evil eye, which didn't do wonders for my dancing technique. It was a relief to get to the toilet and do the old forehead against the wall routine. The door opened and closed behind me and I braced myself, but the shadow that fell across the tiles could only be one man's.

'Sorry,' said Norman, mid-pee.

'Eh?'

'About your first day. You're not supposed to work the machine that fast when it's a new guy.'

'So it wasn't totally my fault the fish went everywhere?'

He shook his head. 'You did okay,' he said, and almost smiled. It was weird, like a friendly third face trying to emerge from beneath the two serious ones that joined down the front.

'Well if you're really sorry, maybe you could do me a wee favour.'

I went back into the hall with Norman in tow, ready to do his human shield and generally make me look less of a Jimmy No-Mates, but when we saw The Joker sitting next to Michelle, even he seemed to bottle it. 'Maybe this isn't such a good idea,' he said.

'You've got to be four times his size, Norman. I want you to go over there and tell him to give it a by.' Then The Joker started getting heavy with Michelle. 'Ho!' I grabbed his arm. 'Steady the buffs, wee man!'

Suffice to say, for the second time that day I ended up sprawling on the floor. When I sat up holding my jaw, Norman had The Joker in a bear hug, Michelle was greeting, two bouncers were pushing through the crowd and The Joker was saying, 'I'm entitled to speak to the mother of my bairns, am I no?'

The words 'in', 'over' and 'head' sprang to mind.

Me and The Joker were asked to leave and Norman followed us out. He rested one hand on my shoulder and pointed at me with the other. 'This guy's getting caught in the crossfire,' he told The Joker. 'Both of you shake hands noo and get on that bus.'

'Sorry, Muppet,' said The Joker. 'Christmas isnae always an easy time for parents, ken?'

'Tell me about it,' I agreed.

We sat on the Midnight Express discussing Dr Who toys and access issues. Some girls up the back had crackers left over from an office party and we ended up in paper hats, drinking Smirnoff Ice and reading out jokes. The Joker unrolled his and smiled to himself. 'What did one magnet say to the other?' he asked a redhead in a Santa outfit.

'Don't know.'

'I find you very attractive.'

It looked as if The Joker was going to be the one to get lucky at the end of the day. I turned to my own bruised and battered reflection in the window and shrugged. The words 'fair', 'love' and 'war' sprang to mind.

Sheila Templeton

TOTALITY

*11th August 1999. Excitement has been building for several
years now in anticipation of the last total solar eclipse of both
the 20th century and of the Second Millennium. The path of
totality begins in the North Atlantic where the moon's umbral
shadow touches down at 09:31.*

It is the silence I remember. We sat on the terrace
of the Dean Gallery Cafe, waiting for darkness
to eat the sun. *It is dangerous to look directly
into the heart of the sun, its white-brightness,*
you said. So we wore dark glasses and sipped tea
and smiled at each other. It was still light enough
to see the poems we'd written. That was enough.
Then you took two pieces of paper. Graph paper,
why did you always use these small squares?
A legacy from engineering days? And measured,
making a hole with a pencil, holding it so the sun
would contract into one thin white-hot beam, as if
we were trying to start a fire. And we watched,
absorbed, careful, brushing away scone crumbs,
expecting the moon's shadow to edge on to the table,
a nibbling away of light, three minutes of Totality.
Perhaps we didn't concentrate enough on this
external happening, this phenomenon of nature,
for we could detect no change. Our small sphere
of light still burned its mandala on the squared paper.
Yet everything fell silent. Birds too, in a ragged way,
without orchestration. The singing grass held its breath.
All chatter stopped, as we felt the sun's warmth
withdraw into an uneasy, marvellous twilight. You laid
down the sheet of pierced paper and we sat, wordless,
looking at each other across a table in that half light.

Valerie Thornton

PROSPECTING IN PARTICK

It wasn't the dipping flight
of some departing finch,
nor an indeterminable trill
from a wee silhouette on a treetop,
nor a flash of olive and acid yellow
that might have been a greenfinch:

it was right here in White Street
on the pavement at St Peter's
exotic with its scarlet mask,
white cheeks and black cap.
Its eyes were shut, its head slack,
the black, white and gold wings folded.

I laid it in state under the fence
at number 48 and paid my respects
over the weeks as the mites
that burrow and chew spirited it away
leaving, as relics of treasure in Partick,
a tiny gold pinion or two.

Deborah Trayhurn

MANHANDLED BY MEMORY

amongst innocent mountains
you enumerate for us –
if young in Franco's time – ways
to avoid a beating. When
walls are betrayed, men rampage
through university halls
you run – up or down, back or
along; in the library
open a window, throw out
your books, yourself; if trapped, shield
your head with books, charge (without
catching their eyes) or wait while
others are caught, to sneak by –
just some of the ways, you say
you escaped bruises, except

they are there in your eyes, scars
like dead stars, the slash of oars
or the aftermath of wars
scars like bars, or closed doors, like
smashed jars, bleak shores, before which
I long to erect mountains.

Fiona Ritchie Walker

IN THE EVENT OF FIRE

Of course, Roger stopped for his teeth
and we both put on our glasses.
My 32 years of packing for worst-case scenarios
meant we were the only couple
in dressing gowns and slippers.

I noticed all of us women had brought our bags.
No point in leaving them for easy pickings.
The assembly point was the car park
overlooking the sea. A man tried to photograph
the moon's reflection with his mobile phone.

Next to him, a girl shivered, an oversize leather jacket
slung over her shoulders.
When he offered her a cigarette,
I saw silver glint on her wrist,
an open handcuff spinning.

Back in our room, Roger said
there was no point in calling the police,
it was just some adult fun.
He made chocolate to help me sleep,
had to rouse me just before nine.

I'd dreamt I was a ballerina,
my legs arabesque, raised arms aching.
Packing after breakfast I cricked my back
looking for the dressing gown cords,
nowhere to be found.

Janette Walkinshaw

I'LL SETTLE FOR ARRAN

Planning for the holiday started one morning early, when the shadows were still long and there was a suggestion of mist over the garden. Marjorie was settled in her usual chair in the conservatory where she spent most of her time now.

'What I would like is a walking holiday in France,' she said.

Alec sat in the other chair bending over to tie the laces on his outdoor shoes.

'Why France?'

'Sunshine,' she said. 'Lavender fields. Chestnut trees. Elizabeth David food.'

He placed his slippers side by side beneath his chair and straightened up. 'You know I don't like the heat.'

Marjorie didn't answer him. She leaned back in the chair and closed her eyes, the better to picture the Dordogne landscape, no, the Languedoc. She murmured the word, rolling it round on her tongue. Languedoc. She had never been to France.

'Some seasons of the year will be cooler than others.'

'I'm going for the paper and rolls. Do you want anything else?'

He asked this every morning.

Velvet nights. Velvet nights and the chirrup of cicadas.

*

'Your father doesn't think a walking holiday in France is a good idea,' she told Fiona, who had come to lunch with Derek as they did every Sunday.

'It's what I would like to do. Do you remember the walking holidays we had when you were young? He carried you in a sling in front of him. You counterbalanced the rucksack. People used to smile at us on the hills. I would have left you with your grandmother but he wouldn't hear of it. We loved the hills in those days. We never went abroad.'

Derek had picked up a magazine and was turning the pages but Marjorie could see that he was not reading, but listening to their conversation. Alec was pretending to be asleep.

Fiona laughed. 'Put me off for life, that did. Thank God you stopped as soon as I became too heavy to carry.'

'You don't remember it,' said Marjorie. 'You were much too young.'

'Doesn't matter if I remember or not. There's the photos to prove it. Mostly on Arran. It was dangerous. Supposing he'd fallen on his face. He could have crushed me to death. Or overbalanced on a ridge. Or anything.'

'He wouldn't have. He would now, of course. Our days for ridge walking are over. But walking in France would be nice.'

'We can't afford it,' said Alec, who obviously was not asleep at all.

'Another thing I would like,' said Marjorie, 'would be for you two to get married.'

Derek cleared his throat and concentrated on the page in front of him.

They wouldn't dare answer her back, she knew that. Fiona just muttered, Oh Mum, under her breath and began to clear away the dirty dishes.

*

The minister had taken to calling regularly. Marjorie was an infrequent churchgoer, Alec not at all, but she was a keen member of the women's meeting and was enthusiastic for the fund-raising side of the church, constantly knitting and crocheting little things for the fetes and sales of work. There had been a falling off in her productivity lately, and it seemed to Marjorie that as she produced fewer of the baby matinee jackets, the more solicitous the minister became.

'Nobody crochets any more,' she told him one day. 'Don't expect me to.'

'I don't expect you to,' he said. 'I'm amazed you kept it going so long. Such beautiful little things.'

'Little,' said Marjorie. 'Little things. Little life.'

'Never say that.'

'I do say it. But I've decided what I want to do. I've changed my mind about France. I'm going to walk the pilgrim way to Compostella.'

'Don't be daft,' said Alec. 'It's a thousand miles.'

'How do you know?'

'I looked it up.'

Marjorie turned to the minister. 'He looked it up so that he could discourage me. That's what he's about these days. Discouragement. Here,' she turned to Alec suddenly. 'Look out my walking boots. They're in the cupboard under the stair. I want to have a look at them. I may need new ones. Go on.'

He rose and went out. She smiled at the minister.

'Mind over matter, eh?'

'That's the spirit,' he said.

Alec came back with a Safeway plastic bag. He took out the boots. There was a pair of socks in them, stuffed in and forgotten, from the last time the boots had been used. The boots hadn't been cleaned and the soles were clogged with dried mud. They were in excellent condition.

'Hardly worn,' said Marjorie, leaning back in her chair, and indicating that Alec could return them to the cupboard. 'They're good enough. I won't have to buy a new pair. See,' she said as Alec came back into the room. 'You won't have that expense. Those'll still do. They'll outlast me.'

'The pilgrim way's too long,' said Alec. 'You have to be reasonable.'

'Something shorter,' said the minister. 'Nearer. Iona?'

Marjorie leaned back in her chair and closed her eyes.

*

They met hill walking, on Schiehallion when Marjorie had a quarrel with the man she was with, and was going down on her own. She stood aside to make way for a man coming up and he stopped, for he saw the tears streaming down her face. Are you all right, he asked and she struggled to smile at him. She had been told she had a lovely smile, and it charmed him, and they continued to talk, and he turned, although he was only one third of the way up, and escorted her back to the car. He told her later it wasn't just her tears. It was the glow in her cheeks and the way the white mist was clinging like a halo round her hair.

She left a note on the windscreen of her now ex-boyfriend's car and went off in Alec's. They went into Dunkeld and sat by the river outside the cathedral and talked and talked. She couldn't remember when they stopped talking, but when she said this to him now, he told her not to be daft.

*

She spent hours at the computer, and found out all the sites which related to pilgrimages or Compostella. She printed off the maps that showed all the routes from all over Europe. True, there wasn't a route from Motherwell but you could start from anywhere. The printouts ran to over a ream of paper.

She made a list of books she wanted and made Alec get them from the library.

'You won't have time to read them,' he told her.

'I'll make the time.'

*

'I have a theory,' she told the minister when he called. 'That pilgrimages in the Middle Ages were no more than an excuse.'

He wasn't going to argue with her and smiled encouragingly so that she continued.

'The Church told them that it was a good thing to do a pilgrimage, and life wasn't too great at home, particularly if they were fed up with their wives and children, and a boss telling them what to do all day, and no surplus income. It was easier just to pack some apples and cheese into your pocket and say you were going on pilgrimage. Who would criticise? So off they went and maybe some did go to where they said they would and maybe some didn't. And maybe some came home, and maybe some didn't. And if they didn't come home who was to say they hadn't died on the way, or on the way back. Easier in those days to escape from a life you didn't want.'

'The Crusades as well,' said the minister.

'Exactly,' said Marjorie.

*

'Santiago is named after a saint,' said Alec, who had been looking through one of the books on his way home from the library.

'That's right. Iago is Spanish for James.'

'But we're Protestant. We don't believe in saints.'

'You never go to church. How can you say what you are.'

'But I'm still a Protestant. What do you want to interest yourself in saints for?'

'I'm not interesting myself in saints. It's the way there I'm interested in. I told you. I want to walk one of those pilgrim ways.'

'It's too long.'

'Well it's a thousand miles. And if you walk ten miles a day you do it in a hundred days. People plan it that way so as to arrive in Santiago just before the feast day. I would have to go a bit slower of course. I could maybe walk five miles a day, so I would take two hundred days to do it, add a quarter as much again for rest days, say two hundred and fifty days, say eight months. Of course I wouldn't particularly bother about being there for the saint's day. That wouldn't matter to me. I don't believe in saints anyway.'

And so she went on planning. She had the weather charts which showed when the weather was best for walking along the various stages of the route, which bits would be too hot in summer and which bits would be too cold in winter. And she made lists of the things which she would take with her, which all had to be packed in one small rucksack, for she wouldn't have the strength to carry a big one, but then being Europe she could wash her T-shirts and knickers every night and they would be dry in the morning.

The cost wouldn't be a problem, she explained to Alec, for the pilgrim houses along the route were free. She couldn't invariably stay in one, for they might be too far apart for that, but it meant she wouldn't have to pay for accommodation every night.

'Not every night, just some nights,' she told him. 'And of course the food there is simple. Cheese and olives and bread. When you're walking a pilgrim way you don't stuff yourself with fancy expensive food.'

She wanted to practise that now, but since Alec did the shopping he ignored her carefully worked-out hand-written lists and just bought mince and fish as usual, and a pizza on Fridays.

*

Fiona and Derek came in one Sunday looking flushed and guilty and Marjorie knew they had been up to something. She found out over their meal.

'Mum,' said Fiona. 'Dad says you're still interested in this trip to Spain you mentioned.'

Marjorie waited.

'We've booked you and Dad on a holiday there. Week after next. Fly from Glasgow, nice hotel, full board, Marbella, you don't have to worry about a thing. It's still quite cool there at this time of year. It's just for five days. You should be all right.'

Marjorie spooned some ratatouille onto a plate and handed it to Derek.

'I don't want to go a holiday to Spain.'

'You said you did.'

'I said I wanted to walk the pilgrim way to Compostella, where the church of Santiago stands. It's not the same thing.'

They finished the meal in silence.

*

The minister held her hand. She was having one of her difficult days and would have liked a bit of silence, but he seemed to think it was his job to rally her.

'Do you believe in miracles?' he asked.

'No, but you do, presumably. It's your job.'

'There's miracles and miracles.'

'To get to be a saint, you have to have worked miracles. At least nowadays. Probably the same in the Middle Ages.'

'Bigger and better miracles in those days. In those days you could.'

'People were more gullible then.'

'Or they saw more clearly,' said the minister. 'But you don't believe in miracles.'

'I know. You just wondered.'

'Alec tells me you're making preparations to go to Spain.'

'He is. They are. I wasn't consulted.'

'They thought that was what you wanted.'

'They got it wrong. As usual. All my life people have been getting it wrong.'

*

She pretended to be in greater pain than she was. Alec told the children she wasn't strong enough to go to Spain, so Fiona and Derek took time off their work and used the holiday instead so as not to lose their deposit. Before they went Fiona kissed her mother and said, 'Look after yourself. We'll take lots of pictures and tell you all about it when we get back.'

*

Marjorie lay in bed. Alec sat in a chair beside her, occasionally turning the pages of the *Daily Record*.

But she wasn't asleep. Gently she reached out a hand and touched his. He glanced up and squeezed her fingers and then returned to his newspaper. She sighed.

'Did you clean my boots?' she asked presently.

'Yes.'

'I'll need them.'

'You're not going anywhere.'

'I am, I am.'

A nun looked in at the door, which was slightly ajar, and went away again.

'I'm not, am I? Going anywhere.'

'No.'

'Oh well.' She turned her head to look out of the window. 'I could settle for Arran. But when you stop dreaming you're dead.'

*

Alec took her ashes to be scattered on Goatfell. It was a long way up, and he was overweight, and he was peching by the time he reached the top, with the help of his daughter and son-in-law.

As he said to them afterwards, over a pint in a pub, he couldn't understand what she had been on about, those last few months. It was the drugs probably. Yes, they all agreed on that, drugs could do funny things to the mind, and ordered another round of drinks.

A CHURCHYARD IN SELIGSTADT

I

The journey to the church was difficult,
because they hadn't put a layer of tar
on the road. It was, after the winter
    weather and the constant wear
    of wheels left by the foresters,
a frozen image in the hardened mud
of the sea's surface when the wind
has whipped it up, a sharp and bitter storm.
    But, after much struggling,
    I finally made my way to

II

the village the local people called
'the joyful town', in words you'd be lucky
to hear in that part of the world now.
    The people packed those words away
    when they left Seligstadt behind,
folk who'd reaped and sown so recently
that I kept imagining I heard
the echo of their voices in the air,
    the tread of their feet on the road.
    In many of the cottages

III

(or so I've read) families appear to live who spoke
a Latin language in the Balkan style.
In many others Gypsies had their home
    (they always swell in number
    when houses are left empty).
They have known such unkindness and contempt
through the years it's hardly a surprise
if they look on the strangers they meet
    with fear, even hostility.
    Once I went to a small village

Christopher Whyte

RÈILIG ANN AN SELIGSTADT

I

Bha e doirbh, an t-astar gus an seo,
bho nach deach còmhdach de theàrr riamh a chur
air an rathad, a dh'fhan, às dèidh siantan
    a' gheamhraidh, is dol null 's a-nall
    nan carbad aig na forsairean,
'na ìomhaigh reòtht' a dh'eabar cruadhaichte
air aodann a' chuain, nuair a bhios a' ghaoth
ga sgiùrsadh suas, 's an cathadh guineach, mìn.
    Ràinig mi e, mu dheireadh thall,
    aig ceann gach dìchill 's teannachaidh,

II

an clachan ris am biodh na daoine cantainn
'clachan an àigh', ann an cànain nach eil
an-diugh ga cluinntinn ach gu tearc sa cheàrn.
    Thrèig a' chànan i còmhla ris
    a' chuid a bha ga h-àiteachadh
's ga toirt gu torachas, cho beag air ais,
cha mhòr nach creidcadh tu gum mothaichte
an-còmhnaidh anns an adhar do dh'ath-sheirm
    an guth, 's do dh'ath-aithris an ceum.
    Bha cuid mhath dhe na bothanan,

III

a rèir coltais, le daoin' a' fuireachd annta,
a' bruidhinn cànain Laidinnich air dòigh
nam Balcan, air neo leis na Giofagan,
    a dh'atas an àireamh daonnan
    is taighean gam fàgail falamh.
Nochdadh a leithid a neo-thruacantachd
riutha air fad nan linn, is a tharcais,
bu bheag an t-iongnadh ged a fhreagradh feadhainn
    le nàimhdeas is neo-earbsa ghairg.
    Uaireigin, ann an clachan nach

IV

where the houses had all been abandoned,
only to be chased away by lads
(the stones they threw expressed better than words
　　　the distrust and fear they felt
　　　when confronted by strangers).
But everything was calm in Seligstadt,
and so I'd time to climb up to the church,
and greet the men who were hard at work,
　　　busily repairing the old manse
　　　that was now abandoned, empty.

V

It could have been a fort, not a church,
the building that looked down on those below.
It stood high up on a rising slope,
　　　defensive walls encircled it,
　　　though they were hardly very tall.
A neat lawn lay beyond. The real defence
was provided by the church itself,
strong and sturdy with no opening
　　　or window anywhere at all.
　　　High above hung a gallery

VI

that seemed unsteady, from which the peasants
would loose their arrows on the Turks below
when they were besieged. The men, women
　　　and children from the nearby farms
　　　would come to seek sanctuary
in the church, which soon became for them
a bastion, a castle, their salvation.
The platform had been made from planks of wood
　　　darkened with the passing of time;
　　　you could still see the apertures

IV

robh ach 'na dhìthreabh fhathast, b' fheudar dhomh
teicheadh, 's na balaich a' tilgeil am ionnsaigh
dhèideagan a chuir an cèill gu pongail
    a' ghràin 's an t-eagal a bha iad
    a' faireachdainn ro shrainnsearan.
Ach bha a h-uile rud air dòigh an seo.
B' urrainn dhomh streap suas gus an eaglais,
's mo bheannachd a thoirt do gach obraiche
    bha trang ag ath-thogail an taigh'
    a bh' aig a' mhinistear a bh' ann.

V

Cha b' fhurast' a shònrachadh am b' eaglais e
no daingneach a bh' air a bhith san togalach
a sheas air àird an leothaid chais, cuartaicht'
    le cearcall-dìon de bhallachan
    nach robh ach ìosal, 'nam meadhan
lèanag chuimir. Bha an dìon fìor ga thoirt
le ballachan na h-eaglaise, 's iad smachdail,
àrdanach, gun lorg air fosgladh no air
    uinneig ann an leum an èirigh.
    Os an cionn bha lobht' a' crochadh

VI

's i cugallach, neo-sheasmhach, far am biodh
na tuathanaich a' losgadh air na Turcaich
aig àm nan sèiste. Bhitheadh boireannaich,
    fir is clann an fhearainn mun cuairt
    a' ruith gus tèarmann a shireadh
ann am broinn na h-eaglaise. Dh'fhàs i
'na daingneach làidir gus an sàbhaladh.
Rinneadh an lobhta le dèileachan fiodha
    a dh'fhàs dorch le sàrachadh tìm,
    ach chitheadh tu fhathast gach beàrn

VII
they used to unleash deadly missiles
on those below, exploding, killing many.
The church's roof was narrow and uneven,
    and covered with tiles that recalled
    the curling shape of a cat's tongue.
The years' passing turned them into a long
and fascinating book describing how
colour changes, deepens and develops:
    green, orange, grey, brown and yellow.
    A painter could become entranced

VIII
studying what that book had to teach him,
standing at the canvas day by day,
he could fill an encyclopedia
    with the wealth of knowledge he gleaned,
    as winter gave way to spring,
spring gave way to autumn, and he saw
new colours, different tones, pigments and shades
he'd try to capture and then reproduce.
    But it was the modest graveyard
    behind the grand church that taught me

IX
the most useful lesson. While I was still
climbing I could see all around me
how the hills, through the eight centuries
    since the Saxons had arrived
    had been re-shaped, layer after layer,
the rows and rows of vines they cultivated
increasing every year. The settlers brought,
along with their Germanic language,
    the plants and the expertise,
    knowledge of how the wine matured

VII
bhon a b' àbhaist do na h-urchairean
creuchdach, bàsmhor bhith tighinn 'nan spreadhadh.
Bha mullach na h-eaglaise, 's e corrach,
    caol, còmhdaichte le crèadh-leacan
    air cumadh teangannan nan cat.
Rinn dol seachad nam bliadhna teagasg dhiubh,
's e fada, tàlaidheach, mu dheidhinn gach
atharrachaidh a ghabhas innleachadh
    air an uain', an orains, a' ghlas,
    an donn 's a' bhuidhe. Bhiodh peantair

VIII
dol às a chiall a' beachdachadh air teagasg
a' mhullaich ud, no dh'fhanadh e 'na sheasamh
ron chanabhas, air an rèidhlean, là seach là,
    a' cur uile fhoghlaim ri chèil',
    a' mothachadh, 's na h-earraichean
a' tighinn, leis na fogharan 'nan dèidh,
do dhath ùr, no do dh'inbhe ùr a dhatha,
a' feuchainn ri mhac-shamhlachadh 's a ghlacadh.
    Ach b' ann san rèilig iriosal
    air cùl na h-eaglais' a fhuair mi

IX
teagasg na b' fheumaile. Fhad 's a bha mi
fhathast a' streap, chìte mu thimcheall orm
mar a chaidh na cnuic, air feadh nan ochd
    linntean às dèidh don cheàrn a bhith
    ga tuineachadh, ath-chumadh gus
còmhnard seach còmhnard, far am biodh cruinn-fhìona
a' cinntinn 'nam pailteas. Thug na tuinichean,
còmhla ris a' chainnt Ghearmailtich aca,
    an lus, 's eòlas air deasachadh
    an fhìona, is air mar a thèid

X
in the darkness of the cellars. The king
of Hungary had asked them to come.
They left their mark on the face of that land,
        that they could almost call their home.
        Each generation that followed,
was born and brought up there. The Reformation
came, and they embraced the faith of Luther.
Tolerance thrived among the peoples
        of 'the land beyond the forests',
        where three faiths dwelt side by side

XI
(though the weakest and the poorest group,
who finally became more numerous
than any other, were marginalised).
        Their churches have outlasted them,
        as have the altars and frescoes
they came before in communion and praise.
I read upon those silent, humble stones,
flowers growing here and there among them
        (no one knew the hand that planted
        or tended them), the names of

XII
the luckiest among them, German names.
Where they had made their home they found their rest.
A different fate befell their descendants
        in the twentieth century.
        They suffered three banishments.
Some listened to the hateful, bitter lies
of the Nazis, and began to march
up and down in the foolish uniforms
        of the Hitler youth, believing
        the Jews and Gypsies were lesser

X

a thasgadh anns na seilearan. Ghabh iad
cuireadh bho rìgh na h-Ungair, is dh'fhàg iad
an lorg fhèin air aodann na tìr', a dh'fhàs,
    ach beag, gu bhith 'nan dachaigh fhèin,
    oir b' ann an seo a fhuair gach àl
a lean am breith is an àrach òg. Aig àm
an Ath-leasachaidh, thug iad creideamh
Luther a-steach, agus shoirbhich e leotha,
    san fhearann taobh thall nam fàsach,
    ceadachas a thoirt gu trianaid

XI

de chreideamhan (ach chaidh, mo chreach, an sliochd
na bu laig' 's na bu thruaighe, ach a dh'fhàsadh
mu dheireadh thall nas lìonmhoire 's nas neartmhoir'
    na càch, fhàgail ri taobh). Mar sin
    dh'fhan na h-eaglaisean, 's a-staigh orr'
dh'fhan na h-altairean 's na freasgan. Leugh mi
air na lic uaghach ìosal, umhal, flùr
no dhà an siud 's an seo cinntinn 'nam measg,
    gun fhios air dè an làmh a chuir
    no dh'àraich iad, ainmean na cuid

XII

a b' fhortanaiche, ainmean Gearmailteach.
Fhuair iad tiodhlacadh is fois an tìr
an roghainn. Bha dàn eil' aig an luchd-dàimh
    san fhicheadamh linn. Chuimhnich mi
    air na trì fuadaichean a lean.
Dh'èist feadhainn ri meallaidhean buaireasach
nan Nàsach, 's thòisich iad a' dèanamh màrsail
suas is sìos an èideadh amaideach
    comann nan òigear. B' àill leotha
    creidsinn gu robh na h-Iùdhaich is

XIII

than they; animals, less than human.
When the Red Army came to the region
they fled north with all they could carry
        towards the sorry remnants of
        the empire of that vapid dream.
Those that remained had to pay the price
for every madness, every crime, even
those they had not committed themselves.
        The men and women were herded
        like cattle onto carriages

XIV

and taken to Russia where they were used
as workers, not really much more than slaves,
until the victors' resentment and rage
        began, slowly, to dissipate.
        Those who had sworn loyalty,
as was right, to the Romanian king,
and served in his army, received word
that with a new day they had a new
        enemy. They were not now
        to fight against the Bolsheviks,

XV

as they had done until that morning,
but with the Germans. When they made it home
after the war, many of them were spared.
        They became a sacrifice
        in the final banishment,
perhaps the strangest and most shameful.
They were sold by the dictatorship
of Ceauşescu, one by one, because
        he put a price on each of them,
        and got all the gold he could want

XIII
na Giofagan 'nan sliochdan ìochdarach.
'S an t-Arm Dearg air taomadh anns a' cheàrn,
theich iad leis na b' urrainn dhaibh a ghiùlan
    mu thuath, a dh'ionnsaigh fuidheall bochd
    ìompaireachd an aisling baoithe.
Na dh'fhan den àl, b' fheudar dhaibh gach uile
cuthach is eucoir a phàigheadh, gu ruig
eucoirean nach do ghnìomhaich iad fhèin.
    Chuireadh na boireannaich 's na fir
    air trèanaichean, air dòigh nan sprèidh.

XIV
Thugadh iad gus an Ruis, dh'ùisnicheadh iad
mar obraichean, cha mhòr nach b' ann mar thràillean,
mus tàinig lùghdachadh air mì-rùn mòr,
    air corraich 's ciùrradh, nam buadhair.
    Na bha air bòid na dìlse thoirt,
mar a bu chòir, do rìgh Romàinia,
's a rinn seirbheis 'na armailt, fhuair iad fios
bho là gu latha eile nàmhaid ùr
    a bhith aca. Cha b' fheudar dhaibh
    bhith còmhrag ris na Boilseabhaich,

XV
mar a rinneadh gus a' mhadainn ud,
ach ris na Gearmailtich. An dèidh dhaibh tighinn
dhachaigh, bha cuid mhath dhiubh air an caomhnadh.
    B' urrainn don fheadhainn sin a mhair
    fàs 'nan ìobairt don treas fuadach,
fear bu neònaiche 's bu mhaslaiche, 's dòcha.
Reiceadh iadsan a reic le deachdaireachd
Ceauşescu, ceann seach ceann, oir thugadh prìs
    air gach fear leis an laoch mhòrail,
    is fhuair e làn a rùin de dh'òr

XVI
from the German Federal Republic
who took them in. So many reflections
could have come to my mind as I stood there:
        the history of clearances
        in my country, the wretchedness
of the empty homes, the fine language
that won't be heard again in those districts,
the brutality with which the crofters
        were sent to foreign countries,
        the pain that was in their hearts,

XVII
how difficult they found it to adapt
to their new lives. But with all the beauty
of that place, the peace and fruitfulness
        that I saw all around me,
        though there was also poverty,
I felt not bitterness or anger
but longing and sadness. For I had seen
proof, in a churchyard in Seligstadt,
        of a principle that has spread
        for two centuries in Europe:

XVIII
that everyone who speaks the same language
should live within the borders of one state,
where only that one language will be used;
        where there will only be one
        culture; that different people
cannot live together peacefully
without strife, violence or banishment.
As I looked upon those graves, I thought
        that doctrine wrong and foolish,
        a shame – a scar – a wound.

Translated by Niall O'Gallagher

XVI
bho phoblachd chùmhnantach na Gearmailte
gu bhith gan liùbhradh. Nach iomadh beachdachadh
dh'fhaodadh tighinn gum aigne aig an àm -
'chuimhn' air na fàsaichean lìonmhor
'nam dhùthaich fhìn, air dìblidheachd
nan làrach falamh, cuimireachd na cainnt
nach cluinnear gu bràth anns na ceàrnan sin,
a' bhuirbe leis an deach na tuathanaich
fhuadachadh gu tìrean cèine,
an cràdh a bha 'nan cridheachan,

XVII
cho deacair 's a bha an ath-ghnàthachadh
san t-suidheachadh ùr. Ach le bòidhichid
an àite, leis a' chiùin' 's an torachas
a chunnaic mi mu thimcheall orm,
ged a bha bochdainn cuideachd ann,
cha nimh no fearg a bha mi fidreachdainn,
ach cianalas is bròn. Oir thachair orm
dearbhadh, ann an rèilig an Seligstadt,
prionnsabail a tha ga sgaoileadh
o chionn dà linn air feadh na h-Eòrp':

XVIII
gum bu chòir a h-uile duin' a bhruidhneas
an aon chànan bhith fuireach taobh a-staigh
crìochan aon stàite, far nach cleachdar ach
a' chànan sin, is far nach bi
ach aon chultar ga àiteachadh,
do bhrìgh 's nach urrainn do dhaoin' eadar-dhealaicht'
bhith dèiligeadh gu sìothchail, ciùin le chèile.
'S mi sealltainn air na h-uaighean, smaoinich mi
gur gòrach, ceàrr an teagasg ud,
gur lochdach agus dona e.

Sue Wilson

COUNTERCURRENTS

Leaning over the edge of the dam, Sonia and Alastair watched the huge jet of water plunging from under their feet, a peat-brown flying buttress thundering into the loch far below.

'The baddie has to end up going down there,' said Alastair.

'Definitely,' Sonia said. 'Almost at the end. We see him falling, do the big death-scream fade thing – but we never actually see his body.'

'Then he pops up again somehow for the surprise last-ditch showdown, before the hero finally kills him.'

Sonia glanced round at the flat expanse of water lapping beneath the rear parapet. 'So we couldn't actually have him going right through,' she said. 'He'd have to just fall off the front, or he'd get totally minced in the turbine.'

'Don't be daft – it's an action movie. That's a money shot, that is: the current sucking him in, with him trying desperately to swim the other way, then getting shot out the other side: nobody cares if it's realistic. I'm just not sure we need that final-ambush thing – maybe just the good old spectacular comeuppance and have done with it. Then we could have him getting minced. It just depends how schlocky we want to be.'

'As long as we have the bit where the hero escapes up the salmon ladder.'

'Oh, absolutely. That's a deal-breaker.'

Sonia was a community education worker, Alastair the IT manager for a marketing company, but they'd watched a lot of films together. Envisaging new places as potential locations was an established line of banter. As he often did these days, though, he'd quickly lost sight of their original pitch – a low-budget, comic-noir thriller, cunningly making the most of the resources on their doorstep – in pursuit of blockbuster appeal.

*

Apart from the dam, their weekend destination wasn't living up to the area's picturesque repute – not that the prevailing misty rain, or rainy mist, was doing it any favours. November was a stupid time to go away, especially without a car, but they hadn't managed a proper holiday that year, and both needed a break before they could even start contemplating Christmas. They'd been lucky before, just picking somewhere they'd heard was nice, booking last minute, coming home feeling blessed by off-season sunshine.

On its website, the hotel's home page showed a gracious Victorian stone frontage, which was now dwarfed by a jumble of pebbledashed metastases, extending along the street and out the back. The open fire in another photo, ringed by smiling people raising glasses in comfy armchairs, turned out to be a gas-fuelled ornament in the chilly, beige-painted lobby, where no one was likely to linger.

After arriving from the station the previous night, Sonia and Alastair had wheeled their cases down a succession of Artexed, sharp-angled corridors, joking about leaving a trail of crumbs. 'Probably wouldn't be much point,' Alastair said. 'The mice would have them long before we made it back.'

'Don't,' Sonia said. 'It can't be that bad.'

They finally reached the Garden Annexe, overlooking the coach park, only to find they'd been given a twin room, and had to retrace all their steps.

'Hopefully we'll end up in a bit that doesn't smell of pee,' Sonia whispered, as the Polish receptionist jabbed sullenly at her computer keyboard.

'Maybe we'll get really lucky, and end up in a different hotel,' Alastair said. 'Or we could of course end up standing here all night. That IBM she's got should be in a bloody museum.'

They were dispatched to a double room eventually, although not until the manager had been summoned to conjure it from the booking system, managing to convey disapproval rather than apology as he insisted on re-entering both their names – and thus their non-matching surnames – before handing over the key. The Tay Annexe this time, even though the river was a good mile away. 'Do you think they keep a couple of rooms just for show?' Alastair said, surveying the orange nylon bedspread and frilled valance, the cupboard-sized shower-room and toilet, tiled in Germolene pink. 'Just for putting on the website, I mean, but nobody actually gets to stay in them?'

'Maybe they just use pictures of the owners' bit: they must stay in the main house.' Sonia giggled as another idea struck her. 'Or maybe it's the honeymoon suite.'

It was soon apparent that the whole place smelled of pee, masked to varying degrees by cheap air-freshener, apart from the glaringly lit dining-room, which smelled of stale fish. Sonia and Alastair were the only table of two amidst serried ranks of pensioners, bussed in for the apparently fabled yearly sale at a local

woollen mill, opening that weekend. The lentil soup and steak pie
– from a ruthlessly streamlined 'Special Sale Menu' – were edible,
but not much more, the portions tailored to old ladies' appetites.

'Three nights for the price of two,' said Alastair, dropping his
fork on his plate. 'Suddenly it seems less of a bargain, somehow.'

It should all have been funny, of course. They'd rewritten
adversity into comedy often enough before, almost welcoming
each successive twist in a chain reaction of bad luck. Times like
that always made great stories afterwards.

'Of course both the pubs *had* to be horrible,' Sonia said, after
they'd sat down in the second one that night, overlooking the
deserted, rainswept high street. She was trying for upbeat, but
had to keep her voice down: the three guys sat along the bar by
themselves were the only other customers, and there was no music
on. The first pub – all the rest being shut for the winter – had
been full of drunk local youth, shouting over a vicious techno
soundtrack. Both buildings retained a handsome historic façade,
behind which each had been refurbished, some time back, with a
contrasting but equal lack of charm.

Alastair didn't seem to feel like playing, though. 'Yeah, well,
we'll just have this pint and go, shall we?' He shivered in the
draught from the window. 'I could do with an early night. It's
been a long week.'

The trouble was, this time it was their own fault. They'd been
talking about an autumn break since August, but just never got
round to arranging anything, until suddenly this was the only
weekend they both had free for the rest of the year. Even then,
Sonia had ended up leaving it to Alastair to find somewhere,
passing up their usual tête-à-tête in front of the computer. Having
invested so very little, she couldn't help thinking, they only had
themselves to blame.

*

They'd woken to more rain, and a predictably dismal breakfast.
Sure enough, too, the town's attractions weren't much augmented
by daylight. The shop windows were filled with vintage flesh-tone
dummies modelling knitwear and waterproofs, the pavements
clogged with arm-in-arm biddies clutching umbrellas, and the
nearby abbey was closed for repairs. But as they ate an early lunch
of lasagne and chips in a striplit wood-effect café, bedecked with
tinsel and noisily crowded with families, Sonia saw that the rain
had stopped. It was still dry when they came out, the clouds even
starting to lift and lighten, perhaps, at least for the time being.

Following the signs along the river, they'd both stopped in their tracks when they rounded a bend and saw the dam, framed on either side by steep banks of trees, backed by layers of hills emerging from the grey beyond. The hulking 1940s concrete centrepiece clearly attested greater exigencies than aesthetics in the minds of its creators, but there was still an implacable majesty about its giant inverted wedge, holding back a whole importunate river.

The sky continued to hint at brightness in the offing, and Alastair took Sonia's hand as they walked back along the gantry, to the viewing window over the turbine room.

'That'd be a great spot for a shootout,' Sonia said, peering down. 'All those pipes and stuff to hide behind.'

'Yeah. Excellent ricochets, too, with all that metal. What d'you reckon about a love-interest, by the way? I suppose we have to have one.'

For Sonia, the salmon ladder was a crowning touch. Amidst all their righteous utilitarianism, yesterday's civil engineers had still factored in the poor fish, battling upstream on their heroic homeward journey. Sonia remembered reading somewhere about a physicist who'd worked out how salmon were able to leap up and over such impossible-seeming waterfalls. The explanation lay in the contrary dynamics of turbulence: upward eddies somehow bouncing back through the main torrent, post-Newtonian energies surfed by ancient fishy instinct. When human intervention made that truly impossible, it seemed only fair to provide alternative safe passage.

It wasn't much to look at from the outside – less of a ladder than a shallow, boxy staircase climbing parallel to the bank, or a scaled-down strip of terraced hillside, inconspicuous against the water's mighty descent. Within, though, lay an ingenious sequence of resting pools, linked by gentler currents, channelling a force just as implacable, in its way. There were viewing windows here, too, along the path on the far side, where you could watch the salmon pausing for breath in the spring. From these, and the drawing on the information board, Sonia concluded that a reasonably sized thriller hero could plausibly scale the dam the same way – it would be a squeeze, but there were air pockets over the pools.

'Tricky to film, though,' she said. 'You'd have to have the cameraman going through backwards first, or something.' She had a notion that the hero could even be female, but was realising it was probably best kept to herself.

'The only trouble with dams,' Alastair said, looking past her at the water endlessly hurtling over the precipice, 'is that everyone always wants them to burst. The minute you see a dam in a film, it's like you're already seeing it bursting, getting blown up or whatever, and then when you don't actually get to see it, which you almost never do, of course, you always feel a bit cheated.'

The sky was darkening again now, the first smirr of rain hitting as they hurried towards town. They had tea and chewy scones in the other café along the high street, then ran through a now-settled downpour back to the hotel. There was meant to be a bar, according to the website, but they could find no sign of it, and so returned to their room, where Alastair watched the football reports while Sonia lay on the bed reading her book, longing to fall asleep but knowing she'd regret it. After dinner (egg mayonnaise, followed by shepherd's pie), once the coach-parties had retired, they watched *Basic Instinct* in the residents' lounge, working their way through most of the bottle of Macallan they'd bought that morning, and all the stem ginger shortbread.

Before crashing out, they did at least come up with a plan for next day, when the forecast was a bit more hopeful. Sonia had picked up a leaflet with a map of easy local walks, among which promises was an hour or so's scenic wending beyond the town, around to a conservation village containing a celebrated ancient pub.

In winter garb, their route proved largely nondescript: low-lying farmland and stretches of trees, fringed with cheap modern houses. The confident purple line on the map bore scant relation to the few signs they found, and they kept having to double back through the wrong nondescript bit. Eventually they fetched up beside a field of young cows, beyond which lay the outlines of their destination, looking picture-postcard as promised, at least from this distance. A stile over the fence, flanked by a footpath marker, invited them across.

'I think we should go that way,' Alastair said, pointing along the road.

'Don't be daft, that's about three times as far. There wouldn't be a sign if we weren't allowed.'

'It's too muddy.'

'It's not that bad. Come on, I'm freezing.'

'I just don't want to walk through those cows, okay? Some of them might be bullocks. I'm going along the road.' He turned away and started walking, leaving her to follow if she chose.

She stared after him a moment, then climbed over into the field, watching her step for cowpats. Some of the cows looked up as she passed, regarding her blankly before they resumed grazing.

She wondered how he'd be when he got to the pub. It might be as if nothing had happened, as if their separate arrivals marked the merest divergence of whim, no bad temper involved. Or it might be the start of the full cold-shoulder treatment, or perhaps some middle distance in between. It would all depend how he chose to play the fact that he'd exposed a weakness.

Near the centre of the field, the path ran past a tumbledown huddle of red-brown stones that she'd taken for derelict farm buildings, but closer up the ruins seemed too old for that, their scattered circular outline too big. Consulting her leaflet, she learned they were the remnants of a mediaeval castle with a Gaelic name, built on a man-made island in the loch that once covered the field. The last people who lived there all died of the plague, half a millennium ago. Their neighbours then fired cannons at the building, reducing it to a funeral pyre. The whole river system and everything must have been totally different back then, Sonia realised, mentally plotting the field in relation to the dam, picturing water all around her.

Mounting the other stile, where the path led into the village, she scanned the curve of the road until she spotted Alastair, his red jacket and the hunchback outline of his rucksack, still a good way off. She waved, but maybe he wasn't looking her way; it was too far to see.

The pub was just over the main street, a whitewashed black-timbered inn that had been welcoming weary travellers since a century before Culloden. Sonia scented the woodsmoke eddying from its chimney. The adjoining kerb was lined with cars, mountain-bikes propped three abreast against the end wall. There were two guys smoking outside, glancing her way. She checked reflexively behind her then set off briskly down the road back towards town, fishing her phone from her pocket to switch it off. She'd be well out of sight round the corner by the time he got there.

*

The dam seemed even louder as she climbed the steps to the gantry, and she saw that another sluice was open, doubling the throughput from yesterday. She leaned over the chest-high barrier, letting the huge rush of water fill her ears, resting her gaze in the maelstrom below. She wondered if he'd realise where she'd gone, but doubted that he'd follow her. She thought they probably wouldn't bother with their free third night. There was a train they could catch in a couple of hours.

Sonia stood up and stretched, taking in the prospect once more before she turned back. Even if it wasn't the season for salmon, at least their monument stood year-round, honouring that epic uphill struggle to mate, spawn and die.

Matthew Wright

GREY AREA

The sea is as black as oil. Worms of light dance and move on its surface, cast from the halogens burning on the pier above, making shadows of the boats that bob gentle. The worms wriggle languid in the inky water and I stare at them dull from the early morning and no coffee inside me to wake me up or make me warm. Our boat rises and falls easy and slow, but we are in a lee on this side and I know it will be worse when we round the corner and the wind is in our face. The diesel engine coughs into life. Even in the dark I see the soot reek and smell the belch from the exhaust before it settles to an idle.

'Wake up! Cast the damn rope!' says Tommy.

I cast the rope, its thick coil kissing the concrete of the pier, and I rub at my fingers feeling the waxy salt grease it left in my hand. I move to get the forward line but Tommy has already done it, grumbling, and he slips back into the wheelhouse and the boat pulls off the pier, the inboard complaining all the way. I am new to the job and there isn't much I do right.

I head into the wheelhouse where the knocking of the engine turns to a plod-plod-plod and we stand together in a humid silence. There is little to see in the blackness from the window. A few lights in the Voe, some buoys flashing and bobbing in the wind. That and white crests on the black sea and spray peppering the glass. One of the side windows is broken, just a small hole, but the wind whistles into my ear so that I pull my hat down to one side to cover it.

'Makes you look a squint head,' says Tommy. He smirks.

The wind is an easterly and causes the boat to hump along the short sharp chop of the waves. Tommy stares out into the night, rough old hands gripping the small wooden wheel, brow furrowed and a tension in the shoulders. Out in the night somewhere is a sandbar. It almost reaches the other side of the Voe, just leaves you a wee channel through.

'It's low tide,' says Tommy.

'Think we'll hit it the night?'

Tommy sets his jaw and his brow pulls down. The sandbar wouldn't do much to the boat, but we would be high and dry. Or we overcompensate and end up nestled in rocks on the opposite side of the voe. Tommy would rather drown. So we chug away in silence as he steers with his tongue between his teeth, occasional glances at the depth sounder, its light casting him in a glow. He's grey now but still a bull of a man. Tattoos creep out from under his boiler suit, the suit itself old and black with grease and feed dust and maybe fish blood. My boiler suit is clean and shiny by comparison, too new looking. My boots are barely scuffed.

And then he relaxes, lets out a long sigh, and settles back.

'So we're passed it then. The sandbar,' I say to him.

'Aye. Were you wanting dropped off?'

A ghost of a smile plays at his lips. I shake my head and put the kettle on the stove and stick coffee in the stained cups. Tommy pulls out his pouch and rolls a fag. I pull mine and roll up too.

'You roll fags like a damn student,' he says. I shrug.

He pulls a string of tobacco from his lip then lights up and puffs away, the glowing tip casting orange on his face and giving it warmth the ghostly depth sounder couldn't. I light too and soon the wheelhouse fills with our warm fog, swirling in the draught from the broken window.

'We got enough feed?'

'A pallet and a half.'

He looks at me hard.

'That enough then is it?' he says.

'It's all we have.' I shrug.

It's easy enough and the old bastard knows it. He keeps staring at me. Then the kettle starts to whistle. I hold his gaze for a pause before I turn to pour the water into our filthy cups and then dollop in milk and sugar. We sip our coffee and we smoke. He grimaces at his cup, shakes his head and pours in more sugar. I can't make coffee right either. We all have our problems. His wife is very pretty and half his age. My old man used to say that half a man's problems he'll make for himself, the rest he'll marry. I'm sure Tommy would agree only I doubt he'll be married much longer.

There is a small glimmer of light to the sky, a greying of the black that had been there before. Sometimes I wish the sun rose and fell like a light switch. I don't like this grey area.

On TV last night they said the universe was still expanding and all the stars were moving away from each other. Eventually the night sky will just be blackness. No stars, just black and empty.

He takes a last draw of his fag and throws it past me, out the hole in the window. The wind catches it and burls it about, a small comet, before dropping it in the sea.

The engine churns on. We pass the mooring buoys of other fish farms, their lights winking from the top of their yellow crosses. The lights flash in a sequence that will tell you things if you know how to read them. I don't.

In the greying world I can make out our boat. I can see the pallets of fish feed in their covers, the Palfinger crane at the back, the hauler at the side. Our feed cannon stands like some robot in the gloom, a big square dalek. The poke net and the feed scoops lie beneath. There is the smell of diesel fumes and fish feed and the sea.

I can see the cages now too, lying like wedding rings, flexing and surfing in the choppy waters. Tommy takes a wide berth and manoeuvres in around the anchor lines of the grid. I scuttle out as the boat shores up perfect against the cages, just as he gives it a little squirt of reverse to bring the stern in. I put the forward rope on first; just give it a loop and a couple of hitches on the peg. I run to get the stern rope. There is no cleat for this one so I tie a round turn and two half hitches to the hand rail. The boat goes to idle and Tommy stalks out of the wheelhouse. He checks the forward rope first and then the stern. He looks at the stern's knot. Then he looks at me and then back to the knot. He shakes his head. Then he unties my knot, slackens the boat off and reties it. I just watch.

'There was nothing wrong with that knot,' I say.

He pushes past me and he's pretending not to hear.

'There was nothing wrong with that knot, man.' I say this louder.

'You want to swim for the boat when she takes off, that's up to you,' he says but he doesn't look me in the eye.

Something burns in my guts. It's burnt there a couple of times in this job. The way I am, you're meant to just stick with the embers. Nobody likes a fire.

I have a quick look over the rail. I look at our bonny fish. They recognise us, they know the boat's sound and they know when they will be fed, so they come to the surface. There is a ripple within the pen, like a tide made of salmon on the surface. Underneath the black water they're silver darts. They are a thousand tiny meteors in the blackness, a thousand hungry stars. Whatever Tommy is, he grows a good fish.

He is back having another coffee in the wheelhouse. He has switched on the pump for the feed cannon.

'Dump it in,' he says at my side.

I dump the feed into the hopper of the cannon. It's charged and ready to go. He throws the lever and the water starts pumping through it throwing a fine waterfall onto the cage. Then he throws the other lever and the feed starts tumbling in, pushed into the air by the water that's pumping through the cannon. The cannon roars and the pellets and the water blow through the air like leaves on the breeze and pepper the surface just bonny as the fish begin to boil to get through and taste it. But you can see the jet of it fraying in the wind, rainbows flying as the light battles its way through the mist. He lets the feed fly, and then takes his hand off the lever, watches the fish, sees what they're doing. Then he blasts again. The hopper gets close to empty, but I see it, I'm already hefting the bag of feed from the pallet and setting it up. I slit the bag just as he's finishing the hopper. I work the feed bag over, sluice it into the hopper, jangle the ends of it to get every pellet out. Then I wrap the bag into a tight roll and stow it behind the deck rail, and that way we can keep count. Then he starts the spray again, in and out, in and out, and the rainbow's catching the sunlight as we work. And I keep grabbing the feed bags, cutting them and feeding the machine as it roars and spews feed and water at our hungry fish. And it goes on like that until we are in a rhythm, the machine, the boat and us and the fish. And then it's just work and you don't notice the time or how much you're doing until Tommy shouts:

'How many bags?'

'Eight.'

And he nods, and you can see the fish are getting sleepy now, not so interested. He growls the machine down, and tosses a couple of handfuls at the salmon. They swim at it lazy, interested enough to maybe have a snap, but they aren't so hungry.

Tommy shrugs.

'Eight bags. Write that down.'

So while I'm doing that he hauls out the pump tube and unties the ropes. We are still being blown onto the cage, but the wind is less now, and the sun is up, hazing through the grey cloud and giving us some light. He bustles past me and grabs the wheel. We back up out from the ropes, and then he wheels around the anchor mooring to nose into the next cage over. It wouldn't matter that much if we got our prop fouled but Tommy would hate it. He motors a bit toward the next cage then cuts it to drift up alongside. I get the rope on and he squirts some reverse and I do the knot at the stern. He marches out but he doesn't bother checking the ropes.

'Get the pump in.'

So I slug the pump tube in and then grab a feed bag, cut it and dump it in the hopper. Tommy just stands at it until I'm finished, not looking at me. Then he levers the pump on and then the feed on and we both look at the cage as the fish go wild.

And that's what we do for the morning. The wind dies back and the sun comes out, and we watch the feed in the water and the fish rigorous and healthy flash past as they eat. And for those moments in the cool fresh air, as the fish dance and eat and we stand in the salt and the breeze, and watch the rainbows cast from the feed cannon, for those moments I can't think of a better life than the one I have.

And when the fourth cage is fed we shuffle back into the wheelhouse and sit for coffee, just waiting for the gas ring to boil the kettle. Tommy rolls a fag, so I do too. I roll it fatter this time. We sit and smoke. He sits and he looks at me, an expression I can't read. I look around the place, blow my smoke out the open door.

'You know how they kill the fish at a harvest?' says Tommy.

'Yeah. They put them through a machine. It bumps 'em on the head and stuns them. Then they cut the gills and that bleeds them out so you don't get bloodspots in the fillets.'

'Yeah. That's what they do. They got a new machine now too. Instead of the gills it punches a hole in their throat, hits the artery and bleeds them out.'

He jabs his index finger at his Adam's apple and makes a poomph noise.

'Meant to be a good way of bleeding them.'

'Mmm-hmm.'

'How is your brother?' he says.

I take a good hard draw on my fag. The end glows red and I screw up my face and look at him through the smoke in the wheelhouse, in the sunlight. He is very still. I breathe out and waft the smoke around a bit.

'He's fine.'

'Have you been to see him?'

I nod slowly. He watches me like an owl.

'How is the house?'

'It's fine.'

'How's she?'

I take a long draw again.

'I didn't ask her.'

'But you saw her?'

I nod. The kettle starts to boil, the cap making a hellish shriek as the steam whistles out of it. I wait for him to get it, but he doesn't move, just stares off into space like the noise has switched him off. I shuffle past his knees and switch the gas off. The whistle dies. I make coffee and put the mug down, steaming next to him.

'Ah, what's the point,' he says, and stubs out his fag and sips his coffee.

He doesn't say much else. We eat lunch clumsily in the wheelhouse, rolls and biscuits and more coffee and butter on everything. It's easy to eat and not talk. Then we smoke again. Tommy sighs and stands up, things in him clicking and cracking as he stretches. I yawn and up to follow him. We dawdle outside and survey things like we are important.

'If God had meant things to be easy he would have given us wings,' says Tommy.

'I only need a bottle of whisky to get wings,' I say.

'You need your wings clipped,' he says but he has a half a smile on his jaw and that's a half more than I've seen in a while. And then we're back to work. It's easy. The boat hums and the feed roars into the cages and the fish skelp about the surface, eating and growing and doing life like they had wings themselves. Maybe easier being a fish, even if you do end up on a dinner plate.

When we're finished the sky is glowering again like it wants to get dark and is just waiting for us to get home and about damn time if you ask me. I untie from the last of the cages and we chug back in. It always takes longer going back, that's the way it seems, when you're thinking about home and everything that goes with it. We curl into the harbour and Tommy shores her up against the pier just perfect, and of course I make an arse of the ropes but he doesn't say anything this time, just lets me get on with it and we are both happy with that.

'Well, that's it,' he says.

I take off my life jacket and fire it into the wheelhouse. It jangles around inside, half black with oil.

'Wanting more feed?' I say.

'Ach, we'll do it the morn,' he says. But I think he just wants time to do it himself.

'How's the house?' he says.

'The house is good,' I say.

'How's she?'

'I guess she's fine.' I shrug.

'I really loved that house,' he says.

'It's a nice house,' I say.

'Tell your brother to look after it,' he says.

I nod. I turn to walk away to my car.

'Tell your brother to look after her,' he says behind me, but I pretend not to hear him.

Jean Atkin lives on a smallholding on the edge of the Southern Uplands, and nature, place and history inform her writing. She has had work selected for publication in *Poetry Scotland*, *Southlight*, and *The Eildon Tree*. She won the Dartington Hall Ways With Words Poetry Competition in 2008.

Colin Begg, 36, is a paediatrician from Ayrshire, who has practised medicine from Govan to Gundegai. He is a graduate of the creative writing programmes at UTS (Sydney) and Glasgow University. Colin's poetry and prose has appeared in various magazines and anthologies, including *NWS 24* & *26*. He also co-edits *Gutter* magazine.

Alan Bissett was born in Falkirk and now lives in Glasgow. He is the author of three novels: *Boyracers*, *The Incredible Adam Spark* and, most recently, *Death of a Ladies' Man*. Alan is a full-time novelist and playwright. **www.alanbissett.com**

Kate Blackadder lives in Edinburgh. She was shortlisted for the 2006 *Scotsman*/Orange short story award, won the 2008 Muriel Spark Society short story competition, and was commended in the John Muir Wild Writing Award in 2009. She has had stories published in various women's magazines and has also published poetry.

Isobel Boyle's East African childhood and her Scottish family life lie at the root of her work. She travelled widely with her late husband, and has continued to pursue her love of expeditions with gusto. She recently obtained a BA with the Open University, and lives and works in Glasgow.

David Cameron was born in 1966 and grew up in East Kilbride. His stories were published as *Rousseau Moon* (11:9, 2000); a book of his poems, *All I Saw*, is due to appear. He is married to the glass artist Louise Rice; they live with their two sons in Leitrim, Ireland.

Giles Conisbee lives in Perthshire and often lingers in the sound of the sea. His poems have appeared in magazines such as *Brittle Star*, *Weyfarers*, *Chanticleer*, *Fire*, *Monkey Kettle*, *Inclement*, *The Eildon Tree*, *Rebel Inc.* and *Jednodniówka Literacka*. His debut collection, *Wild Flowers*, was published in October 2008.

Catherine Czerkawska is an award-winning writer of novels, stories, poems, and plays. Her stage play *Wormwood* was produced to critical acclaim at the Traverse Theatre and is a Higher Drama set text. She has just completed a new novel called *The Physic Garden* and a collection of short stories.

John Duffy is a Glaswegian long settled in Huddersfield, where he helped found and run the Albert Poets, a group centred on the pub nearest the library. He works as a bibliotherapist, promoting the love of reading as an aid to well being, and runs writing workshops for community groups.

Rob Ewing is a GP currently living in Barra. His short stories have been published by *New Writing UK, Chapman, Cadenza, Leaf Books, Aesthetica, Slingink, Pushing out the Boat, Northwords Now, Libbon, Outercast,* and performed on BBC Radio Scotland; his poetry has been shortlisted for the William Soutar writing prize. He has just completed a novel set in Victorian-era Scotland and London.

Corinne Fowler branched off into fiction writing after the publication of her first book: *Chasing Tales: travel writing, journalism and the history of British ideas about Afghanistan* (Rodopi, 2007). She has published a number of short stories since then and is co-writing a novel about Paraguay with her twin sister Naomi.

Ewan Gault is 27. 'The Restless Wave' is the opening chapter of a novel he hopes will one day be published. Other chapters have won the Fish Knife/CWA prize in 2007, shortlisted 2008 and runners-up prize in *The Scotsman*/Orange short story competition. He is currently working and writing in Milan.

Diana Hendry's fourth and most recent collection of poetry is *Late Love & Other Whodunnits* (Peterloo/Mariscat). Her short stories have been widely published and broadcast and she has written more than forty books for children. Currently she is a Royal Literary Fund fellow at Edinburgh University.

Kate Hendry teaches English and Creative Writing at Barlinnie prison and for the Open University. Her work has been published in *Harpers, Mslexia, The Reader* and *The Rialto* as well as in previous editions of *New Writing Scotland*. 'The Coop' is from a novel-in-progress. She lives in Ayrshire.

Nick Holdstock's work has appeared in the *Edinburgh Review, Stand,* and *The Southern Review*. He edited the *Stolen Stories* anthology and was shortlisted for the 2009 Willesden Herald Short Story Prize. More information at **www.nickholdstock.com**

Vicki Husband is studying on the Creative Writing Masters course at Glasgow University and works for the NHS. Previous work has appeared in *Mslexia* magazine, *Aesthetica* magazine, *LauraHird.com, Present Poets* and *New Writing Scotland 25*. In 2008 she was a runner-up in the Edwin Morgan International Poetry Competition.

Elisabeth Ingram is currently studying for an MLitt in Creative Writing at Glasgow University. In March 2009 she received a Dewar Arts Award to support her as she writes her first collection of short stories. Elisabeth is a co-editor of Glasgow University's *From Glasgow to Saturn*, and blogs at **iluvwords.blogspot.com**

Kirstin Innes is a journalist, writer, and recipient of the 2008 SAC New Writers Award. She is currently working on her first novel, *Dance Me In*. Kirstin won the 2007 Allen Wright Award for Excellence in Arts Journalism, and has twice been nominated for Feature Writer of the Year at the National Magazine Awards.

Mary Johnston, a native of Aberdeenshire, now lives in Midlothian. Publications include *Teuchat Storm, Smaa Spangs and Ring o Sangs*, and *Kennt His Faither*. A new collection of poems *Fa Dis She Think She Is?* (Calder Press) will be published in 2009. To preserve the sound of the Doric dialect a CD is affixed to each pamphlet.

Bridget Khursheed is a poet. Her work has appeared in publications including *Fire, The Shop, The London Magazine* and *The Rialto*. She has worked as a wholefood collective partner, dotcom pioneer and Anglo-Saxon teacher. She lives in the Scottish Borders with her family. Good on mountains, bad on towers.

Eleanor Livingstone is Artistic Director of StAnza, Scotland's International Poetry Festival. Her publications include *The Last King of Fife* (Happen*Stance*, 2005), *A Sampler* (Happen*Stance*, 2008); and as editor *Skein of Geese* (The Shed Press, 2008) and *Migraasje: Versions in Scots and Shetlandic* (Stravaigers, 2008). **www.poetrypf.co.uk/eleanorlivingstonepage.html**

Rowena M. Love, poet, writer and performer, has had work appear worldwide. *The Chameleon of Happiness* was her first collection; *Comin Oot in the Wash,* a pamphlet of Scots poetry, her latest. In between has been the joint Makar Press collection *Running Threads* and their audiobook entitled *Lip Synch.*

Harry McDonald is a Glasgow-born writer still belonging to Glasgow. He is in the final year of the Glasgow University Creative Writing MLitt course. He is currently working on a collection of short stories. He has previously had poetry published in the SQA Anthology, *Write Times,* and also fiction in *Nerve* magazine.

Joe McInnes graduated from Glasgow University in 2002 with an MA in Literary Studies and in 2008 with a MLitt in Creative Writing. His poetry has been published in *Cutting Teeth* and short stories anthologised in *The Research Club* and *Let's Pretend.* He is currently writing a short story collection.

Dubliner **Ian Macpherson** won the first Time Out Comedy Award in 1988. His books include *Deep Probings, Posterity Now* and *Hortense and Her Sensible Friend.* His one-man shows include *The Chair* and *The Joy Of Death.* 'Salmon Chamareemo' is from the forthcoming collection *How To Survive The Menopause With Your Manhood Intact.*

Andy Manders lives in Perthshire, writing the odd bit poem and story when looking after the bairns, earning a meagre crust and weather permit.

Theresa Muñoz was born in Vancouver in 1983. She has published her poetry widely in Canadian and Scottish magazines, including *Canadian Literature, New Writing Scotland 25, Poetry Scotland* and *The Red Wheelbarrow.* She is currently a PhD candidate in Scottish Literature at the University of Glasgow, Dumfries. She is a regular contributor to the *Sunday Herald's* book pages as well as the *Scottish Review of Books.*

John Murray stays in Kelso and teaches landscape architecture at Edinburgh College of Art. Poems are in *Chapman, The Eildon Tree, Lallans, The New Makars, New Writing Scotland* and *A Tongue in Yer Heid.* Diehard published a first anthology, *Chiaroscuro.* A collection about the River Teviot is in *Tweed Rivers.*

Liz Niven is a poet and creative writing tutor. Originally from Glasgow, she's based in Dumfries. She has published several poetry collections in English and in Scots, including *Stravaigin* and, most recently, *Burning Whins*, and has participated in a range of international literary events. **www.lizniven.com**

Ronnie Nixon lives in Glasgow. He has previously had poetry published in *New Writing Scotland* 24. He was a runner-up in the 2007 Flosca Short Story Competition, and was the winner of the 2008 Earlyworks Press Short Story Competition.

Niall O'Gallagher is a political reporter for BBC Alba and Radio nan Gàidheal. He has written on Gaelic and Irish poetry for the *Guardian* and the *Herald* and is co-editor, with Pàdraig MacAoidh, of *Sùil air an t-Saoghal* (Clò Ostaig, forthcoming), a collection of essays on modern Gaelic writing. A collection of Gaelic poems is currently in preparation. He lives in Glasgow.

Jane Rawlinson has lived and worked in Aberdeenshire since 1980. She has four published novels, two of which draw on her experience of living and working in Kenya and Iran. Short stories also published in various magazines. She is currently working on a novel, short fiction and poetry.

James Sinclair was born in 1961 in Lerwick, where he works as an engineering storeman. He began writing in his 40s and his poetry pamphlet *Gulf Stream Blues* was published by North Idea in 2007. He has read his work at Wordplay, WORD and Wordfringe Festivals.

Nancy Somerville was born in Glasgow and now lives in Edinburgh. Her poem, 'Bucket of Frogs', was the title poem of *New Writing Scotland* 26 (ASLS, 2008). Her first poetry collection, *Waiting for Zebras*, was published by Red Squirrel Press (Scotland) in 2008.

Gerda Stevenson, actor/writer/director, was awarded a Scottish Arts Council Writer's Bursary (2008). Her poetry has appeared in *The Scotsman, Cencrastus, The Eildon Tree, Parnassus: Poetry in Review* (New York), *Cleave* (Two Ravens Press), and *Aesthetica Magazine*. Her many BBC Radio 4 dramatisations include *The Heart of Midlothian* and *Sunset Song*.
www.gerdastevenson.co.uk

Andrew Stott grew up on a farm in the Scottish Borders and has lived in Edinburgh all of his adult life. He has been writing consistently for the last two years and is in discussion with an agent over his first novel.

Alison Swinfen lives and works in Glasgow and is a member of the Iona Community. Her first collection of poetry, *Through Wood*, appeared in 2009 (Wild Goose Publications).

Daryl Tayar lives in Glasgow with his wife and two boys. He writes poetry, children's fiction and dictionaries, doing all he can to raise awareness of climate change and to explore both his inner landscape and this disintegrating world – passing on what he's hauled from the oblivious darkness of daily life.

Jim Taylor is from Glasgow but now lives in Shetland. He has had stories in *Chapman*, *Edinburgh Review*, *Rebel Inc.*, *West Coast Magazine*, *New Writing Scotland* and *New Shetlander*. 'The Muppet Show on Ice' is taken from a recently completed novel.

Sheila Templeton lives by the sea in Ayrshire. She writes in English and Scots and has had poems published in a collection, anthologies, magazines and newspapers, as well as winning the McLellan and McCash Poetry Awards. At present she is working as Poet in Residence at the Harbour Arts Centre Irvine.

Valerie Thornton is a writer, an editor and a creative writing tutor. She has held two Royal Literary Fund Writing Fellowships at Glasgow University. Her tutoring embraces mainstream and specialist groups, and the Open University. Her latest creative-writing textbooks are *The Writer's Craft* and *The Young Writer's Craft* (Hodder Gibson).

Deborah Trayhurn trained as a painter. At some point the jottings in the margins of drawings acquired a life of their own. With her family, moved frequently, in each new landscape, or friend, found fresh inspiration. Now settled in Perthshire, where the terrain provides an expansive canvas for exploring thought.

Janette Walkinshaw is privileged to live in Galloway. She has had plays and short stories broadcast on Radio 4 and short stories in various anthologies and magazines. Her work is either very funny or very miserable and until she's finished a piece she never knows which it is.

Christopher Whyte is a prize-winning poet in Gaelic and the author of four novels in English. His third collection, *Dealbh Athar*, was published by Coiscéim of Dublin this spring, and a fourth collection in Gaelic and English, *Bho Leabhar-Latha Maria Malibran / From the diary of Maria Malibran*, will be published by Acair of Stornoway in autumn 2009. He lives in Budapest and writes full-time.

Freelance arts journalist **Sue Wilson** writes regularly for a variety of publications, including the *Scotsman*, the *Sunday Herald*, *Metro* and *Songlines* magazine, and is co-author of *The Rough Guide to Irish Music*. She completed an MLitt in Creative Writing at Glasgow University in 2008, and is currently working on a novel.

Matthew Wright is from Kirkwall, but now lives in Shetland. He wrote 'Topping Up', a pamphlet published by North Idea, and recently won a runner up award in the Bridport prize. He used to be rock'n'roll but then just lost it. It wasn't in the last place he looked.